The Year's Work in Medievalism

Edited by M. J. Toswell

XXII
2008

WIPF & STOCK · Eugene, Oregon

The Year's Work in Medievalism
Series Editor, Gwendolyn Morgan

The Year's Work in Medievalism, volume XXII, is based upon the proceedings of the International Conference on Medievalism for the International Society for the Study of Medievalism. The conference, held at the University of Western Ontario, was supported by the Social Science and Humanities Research Council of Canada. The principal organizer, and the editor of this volume, is M.J. Toswell. *The Year's Work in Medievalism* also publishes bibliographies, book reviews, and announcements of conferences and other events.

The 2008 volume is indexed in *The Modern Language Association International Bibliography.*

Copyright © *Studies in Medievalism* 2009

ISBN 978-1-55635-959-0

First published in 2009 by Wipf and Stock Publishers
199 West 8th Ave., Suite 3
Eugene, OR 97401
Web site: www.wipfandstock.com
for *Studies in Medievalism*

The Year's Work in Medievalism is an imprint of *Studies in Medievalism.* For volume XXII in particular, write M.J. Toswell, Editor, *The Year's Work in Medievalism,* Dept. of English, University of Western Ontario, London, Ontario, Canada N6A 3K7. For the series generally, write Gwendolyn Morgan, Editor, *The Year's Work in Medievalism,* Department of English, Montana State University, Bozeman, MT 59717.

The Year's Work in Medievalism
Volume XXII 2008

Introduction

M.J. Toswell

The Call for Papers for the 22nd annual conference of the International Society for Studies in Medievalism asked for papers which would address "neomedievalisms."[1] More specifically the call quoted Umberto Eco's famous dictum about how today we exist in "a period of renewed interest in the Middle Ages, with a curious oscillation between fantastic neomedievalism and responsible philological examination" (63). The result, Eco argued, was the modern desire to "dream the Middle Ages." On one level our desire works to return us to our roots, to find our origins, on another our desire makes the Middle Ages anew, makes the medieval period happen the way it ought to have according to the individual modern re-conception—or preconception. Neomedievalism is therefore, the call for papers noted, a polysemous term referring for political scientists to a return to barbaric nation-states or tribalism; for media theorists to video games, graphic novels, and other modern media which reconceptualize the medieval; for traditional medievalists to the historiography of the discipline, the way in which our conception of the medieval depends so profoundly on former scholars and their hopes and desires, their failings and their strengths; and for many others, to an interdisciplinary category which includes all the above and any new approach to the medieval in the past five centuries, now leaning into the sixth. In short, the call for papers proposed a very broad range of definitions for neomedievalism and for the neomedievalisms that individual scholars might wish to pursue.

The papers proposed in response to the call varied widely, from careful reconsiderations of Longfellow's Dante to animated interpretations of shopping in medievalist video games, from Meyer Schapiro to Prosper Merimee, from Sir Walter Scott to Ridley Scott, from comic books to Kingsley, from films about the Middle Ages to arguments about what medievalism is, from Tolkien to Morris and back again. The conference itself began with a keynote lecture by Terry Jones, an independent scholar perhaps most famous for his work with the Monty Python troop, who continues to pursue a multivalent career with the writing and direction of movies, serving as presenter for television programs, and writing major monographs on Chaucer and on fourteenth-century politics. His paper anchored the conference and fascinated its audience as he offered a new interpretation of the character of Richard II, and produced substantial evidence for the way in which Henry IV, and more probably Thomas, Bishop of Arundel, had recreated and restructured both the history of Richard's reign and representations of him in the visual and literary arts. He concluded that, contrary to standard opinion, there is no shred of evidence that Richard II was weak, vacillating, unpopular—in short, a tyrant. Conversely, there is evidence that he was not, and evidence that writers and historians went back to change their stories and their approaches to Richard II.

The notion of recreating and reconceptualizing an earlier period carried through into the ensuing plenary papers: Alain Corbellari sieved very carefully through the ways in which Europeans in the mid-twentieth century had constructed their notion of nationhood with careful reference to the empires and nations of the Middle Ages as originary signs of national excellence—a practice notable in Germany but also employed in other European nations. Richard Firth Green considered the post-medieval history of the medieval romance of "Sir Eglamour of Artois," focusing on the ballad called "Sir Lionel" and more recent versions of it from the Appalachian mountains based on song matter now often called "Old Bangum." The papers presented in this volume were all delivered at the conference, and extensively revised in the process of submission and review. They ably represent the ideas that excited the conferees and led to much discussion in the corridors on the way to papers and in the Great Hall at Huron University College in the University of Western Ontario, which was the central gathering place for most of the event. The conference itself, and these proceedings, was sponsored by the Social Sciences and Humanities Research Council of Canada under the aegis of the Aid to Scholarly Conferences and Workshops grant program.[3]

It could well be argued that this very broad approach to medievalism, and especially to neomedievalism, is too simplistic—which it certainly is. It reflects the massive thirst for the Middle Ages that inheres in the modern day, perhaps a thirst for roots and origins, perhaps simply a thirst for simplicity and a clear sense of the order of things, perhaps a more complex engagement with the concepts of tradition and modernity (as Brian Stock would have it) as competing impulses in the postmodern world. The papers in this volume demonstrate various aspects of those competing impulses, and ably demonstrate the continuing centrality of the Middle Ages, through medievalism and neomedievalism, in our postsingular world.

UNIVERSITY OF WESTERN ONTARIO

NOTES

1   The first draft of the call for papers was developed by Michael Kightley. Two particular delights of the conference were the wonderfully playful poster designed by Brice Hall under the supervision of Mario Longtin, and the website at <u>http://www.uwo.ca/english/neomedievalisms</u> designed and administered by Mark McDayter. Kaya Fraser also deserves mention for her fine eye with copy-editing in the production of these papers.

2   See Umberto Eco, "Dreaming of the Middle Ages" 63. Eco's statements, and in particular his list of the ten loosely-defined approaches to reinventing the Middle Ages, have proven to be touchstones in thinking about medievalism; for example, see Frayling, *Strange Landscape*, the book accompanying the BBC series entitled *Strange Landscape*, whose opening chapter considers the Middle Ages today from the point of view of Eco, and whose Appendix 1 lists the ten approaches, and gives Frayling's examples of each one. The book and series were framed within the terms of Eco. A more general approach, but one which may prove to have more staying power, is Hutcheon, *A Theory of Adaptation*, which considers the ways in which stories evolve and mutate in

order to fit "new times and different places"(176); though not specific to medievalism, Hutcheon's theory offers an organic approach rather than one embedded in and always frustrated by a sense of what is the 'right' way to approach the medieval.

3 The Vice-President, Research, at The University of Western Ontario was also very generous with funding.

WORKS CITED

Eco, Umberto. "Dreaming the Middle Ages" *Travels in Hyperreality* trans. William Weaver. San Diego: Harcourt, 1986. 61-72.

Frayling, Christopher. *Strange Landscape: A Journey through the Middle Ages.* London: Penguin and BBC Books, 1995.

Hutcheon, Linda. *A Theory of Adaptation.* New York: Routledge, 2006.

Jones, Terry. *Chaucer's Knight: The portrait of a medieval mercenary.* London: Weidenfeld and Nicolson, 1980.

_____. "Was Richard II a Tyrant? Richard's Use of the Books of Rules for Princes." in Nigel Saul, ed. *Fourteenth Century England* vol. 5. Woodbridge: Boydell & Brewer, in press.

_____. *Who Murdered Chaucer? A Medieval Mystery.* London: Methuen, 2003.

Stock, Brian. *Listening for the Text: On the Uses of the Past.* Philadelphia: University of Pennsylvania Press, 1990.

Anxious Medievalism: An American Romance

Amy S. Kaufman

One day, while I was house-hunting in Macon, Georgia, I encountered a very strange neighborhood.[1] It had a guard gate, but it did not appear to be a typical gated community. It was filled with modest ranch-style houses roughly thirty to fifty years old, oversized, "W '04"-stickered pick up trucks parked in red clay driveways, and four-wheelers glittering on overgrown lawns. The residences behind the gates were neither historic homes nor gargantuan McMansions. What then, I wondered, could the inhabitants possibly be guarding?

The sanctity of the enclosure became clear when I started to look at the street names: King Arthur Drive, Galahad Circle, Nimue Lane, and Will Scarlet way, and on and on—an endless array of grand titles that seemed to scream, "medievalism was here!" The only street names that differed were the neighbourhood's two main roads: Rebel Drive and Confederate Lane. This place, I realized, was a veritable suburban monument to American south's most sacred myth, its dream of a chivalric Confederacy. Medievalism thrived at the heart of the southern Confederacy, and there exist today few national memories that rival the south's longing for its Civil War past. The strange juxtaposition of medieval fantasy and Confederate history reflected by that unassuming Georgia neighborhood is the calling card of America's southern states, the very states that are, not coincidentally, also the heartland of the evangelical movement.

The south's history of desire for the past may help to explain the recent medievalism of the American evangelical movement, in which dreams of the past have been performing a great deal of heavy-handed cultural work of late. Evangelical medievalism is manifesting in commercial products like the "Armor of God PJs," which come complete with a plastic sword, a shield, and a red cross emblazoned across the chest of each set of sleepwear; conversion websites such as *E-Sword*: "The Sword of the LORD with an Electronic Edge"; and a variety of supermarket-shelf tomes of wisdom, including: *His Princess: Love Letters from Your King, Raising a Modern-Day Knight,* and *Balancing the Sword: A Comprehensive Study Guide to Life's Manual.*[2] As amusing and innocuous as these examples seem to be, the medievalism of this religious movement is about more than moving a fun product. Much like the medievalism of the south's Civil War ancestors, today's evangelical medievalism is a longing for the past with a purpose. The commercial branch of this movement is marketing a strictly gendered medieval fantasy that desperately wants to validate itself with the weight of history, but requires a masterful revision of that history in order to bear it.

For example, the Christian commercial powerhouse Vision Family Forum hosts an online catalogue that offers two separate sections for children. The first of these is "The *Boy's* Adventure Catalog," (the italics are original to the website), which provides a panoply of medieval-themed paraphernalia under the category of "Chivalrous Boyhood" to entertain young men, including the "William Wallace sword," Lion and Cross Shield sets with which you can train your sons to be "protectors of womankind," and the "Medieval Model Trebuchet."[3] The corresponding "Beautiful *Girlhood* Collection" features dolls, sewing kits, and a CD called *Sleeping Beauty and the Five Questions*, which, as the description of the CD claims,

> challenges fathers on the importance of guarding their daughters' hearts at all costs, how to shield them from the pressures of a peer-oriented society and inappropriate romantic relationships, and how to prepare them as a bride—a godly young woman of purity for the young man of their dreams whom God is preparing.

The grammatical error in which "daughters" become "a bride" is a fine representation of this movement's conflation of all young women into one idealized, passive archetype, as is the difference between the italicized portions of the catalogue pages: *boy's*, a possessive term indicating ownership, and *girlhood*, a passive, preferably beautiful, state of existence. The cover of the *Sleeping Beauty* CD further illustrates both its emphasis on female passivity *and* the revisionism required by its desire for history: the product sports an altered reproduction of Edmund Blair Leighton's "The Accolade," the famous 1901 painting of a medieval damsel knighting a young man who kneels before her. The images have been repositioned on the Vision Forum CD, however, so that the would-be knight looms *over* the damsel, and she appears to be bowing her head to him and holding out her empty hand. Not surprisingly, the formidable blade held by Leighton's damsel has disappeared. Apparently, *fin de siècle* depictions of medieval romance motifs are far too radically feminist for the Vision Family Forum to reproduce accurately.

The American evangelical movement uses such remixes of history, literature, and imagery to justify an edict of strict sexual hierarchy, returning Americans to the 'good old days' of absolute masculine supremacy. The Middle Ages is being seized as that ideal past, a past that seems to offer the cure for what some evangelicals consider an epidemic of passive, effeminate Christian men. John Eldredge, author of the wildly popular treatise on Christian masculinity, *Wild at Heart*, blames the church itself for this crisis. He argues that "Christianity, as it currently exists, has done some terrible things to men. When all is said and done, I think most men in the church believe that God put them on the earth to be a good boy" (7). Being a "good boy," according to Eldredge, is antithetical to real Christian manhood. His answer to the books and talk shows that lament, "Where are all the real men?" is, succinctly, "*You asked them to be women*" (7, original emphasis). What these men really need, according to *Wild at Heart*, is "a deeper understanding of why they long for adventures and battles and a Beauty—and why God made them *just like that*" (xi, original emphasis). As for the Beauty (which Eldredge always designates with a weird capital 'B'), "her childhood dreams of a knight in shining armor coming to rescue her are not girlish fantasies; they are the core of the feminine heart and the life she knows she was made for" (16).

Eldredge is not alone in his anxiety over church men who go 'soft.' Scott Lively, founder of Abiding Truth Ministries, complains in his article "Masculine Christianity" that women far outnumber men in congregations because "the modern American church, along with the majority of its leaders, has rejected masculinity in favor of an effeminate Christianity."[4] Lively issues a "vigorous rebuke to both women and men within the church who reject the masculine side of Christianity," and in particular, "a rebuke to those pastors' wives who keep their shepherd husbands safely close to the flock when they should be sometimes out hunting the bears and wolves." Thanks to activists like Lively and Eldredge, these neglected "shepherd husbands" are being given unprecedented institutional encouragement to reclaim the church as their own. In a 2006 article in *Harper's*, Jeff Sharlet investigated the aggressive political and social agenda of the Evangelical movement and found that it was propelled by a palatable anxiety over the Church's 'masculinity' [33-43]. During his investigation, Sharlet attended a sermon by Pastor Rusty Thomas of Waco, Texas, who asserted that gender trouble was not only at the core of problems in the church, but was responsible for many of the problems in America. "There is a 'mothering' church...and a 'fatherhood' church," Thomas declares. "This nation is too far gone to be redeemed by mercy alone. It is the father church's time" (39). Thomas's "father church" is also fueled by medieval fetish: "The symbol of the state is a sword," Thomas explains, "Not a spoon, feeding the poor, not a teaching instrument of the young....And the sword is an instrument of death!" (qtd in Sharlet 43). Sharlet notes that members of this movement take this symbolism so seriously that they often "gift one another with real blades crafted to medieval standards" (34).

If medievalism is the cure for this movement, then femininity is most certainly the disease. Eldredge, who has encouraged his own sons to be so masculine that they "chew their graham crackers into the shape of handguns at the breakfast table"[10], laments that the contemporary vision of a loving Jesus is just too wimpy: "Mister Rogers with a beard. Telling me to be like him is like telling me to go limp and passive." Eldredge declares, "I'd much rather be told to be like William Wallace"[22] He then spends page after page proving that Jesus is, in fact, *just like* William Wallace (24-9). Eldredge and his cohorts thus locate authentic masculinity, even biblical masculinity (which presumably would have been functional long before William Wallace wielded his sword), directly in the Middle Ages. This anachronistic vision of authentic 'medieval' biblical masculinity is so appealing that it has even permeated the toy department. In the "Almighty Heroes" line of action figures, for instance, biblical celebrities have had a medieval-inspired testosterone-injected makeover. David and Moses even sport plate mail armor over their brawny chests.[5]

The shadow side of this call to arms, of course, is the call for women to return to the shelter of the very feminine spheres of the church that men are encouraged to leave. John Eldredge claims that poor "Beauty" has degenerated for lack of a few good knights. "This world kills a woman's heart," Eldredge explains, "when it tells her to be tough, efficient, and independent"(17). Women have grown "grasping" and manipulative rather than pleasingly vulnerable: "No longer does she want simply to share in the adventure," he whines, "now, she wants to control it....Put simply, [she] is no longer simply *inviting*" (51-2, original italics). The anxious repetition of the word "simple" is at the core of the desire for the medieval in this text; the fantasy at work is that the Middle Ages were simpler times, simpler days, when men were knights and women were "simply inviting." Eldredge goes on to explain the ways in which the modern day knight's chivalrous protection of the Beauty will 'encourage' her to be inviting once again, thus completing the ideal partnership of medieval knight and damsel in distress. Eldredge reveals both the fact that he sees this pair as inextricably symbiotic—masculine agency *depends* upon female passivity—and that his vision of history is deeply skewed when he asks, "What would Robin Hood or King Arthur be without the woman [*sic*] they love?"(15). Once again, the idealized medieval feminine is constructed in the singular, an ideal that is simultaneously deconstructed through comparison to the original model. After all, medieval portrayals of Guinevere as a fickle adulteress certainly indicate that if such a 'simple,' gracious, passive past ever *did* exist for women, the medieval era was not exactly its shining moment.

As Umberto Eco tells us, "the Middle Ages have always been messed up in order to meet the vital requirements of different periods" (68). So what *are* the requirements of this period, of today's evangelical movement in particular, that it should pine for an imaginary time in which God was a real man? In her 2005 study *Hollywood Knights*, Susan Aronstein documents an earlier incarnation of the medieval masculinity phenomenon, the mythopoetic men's movement of the 1980s, which used the Grail legend to "heal" masculinity in a time of perceived crisis. Aronstein argues that this movement viewed the Middle Ages as the "dream of a true patriarchy."[6] Likewise, contemporary evangelical medievalism desires the Middle Ages because it desires an ideal patriarchal past, all the while preaching that male empowerment requires female submission. Stephen Ducat's study of contemporary religious politics, *The Wimp Factor*, offers an explanation for this desire. Ducat points out that these days, "fundamentalists everywhere share a creed that includes the restoration of a fantasized golden age of unfettered patriarchal domination" (208). The source behind this fantasy is what Ducat calls "femiphobia," which is "an unconscious defense that is employed to keep out of mind...an *identification* with women" (1, original emphasis). Fear of the *internal* feminine is articulated in frantic displays of manliness that Ducat terms "anxious masculinity." If we apply Ducat's analysis to the evangelical medievalism fetish, then, it seems reasonable to designate the evangelical longing for the Middle Ages *anxious medievalism*.

Anxious medievalism, like anxious masculinity, is equally unrelenting in its call for female submission because it fears its own internal feminine. In the hyper-homophobic American culture, care-giving and nurturing, qualities that naturally occur in both women and men, must be distorted into armed male "protection" of women, while the desire for homosocial intimacy can only be articulated behind cries for a brotherhood of knights. Anxious medievalism dreams of resurrecting its imaginary, idealized past through a journey "back" to masculinity. This transition can only be guided by fathers, who must teach young knights how to brandish their swords. "Whatever the mother's failure," John Eldredge assures us, "it can be overcome by the father's engagement" (68). This is the ultimate call of *Wild at Heart*: for legions of devoted Christian fathers to recapture "true masculinity," or phallic power, from the feminine and pass it on to their eager sons. After all, when Eldredge confides that the girly-man Jesus makes him "go limp," he reveals the true nature of his anxiety: that today's feminized Christianity *castrates* its followers, and the only way for a Christian man to regain power is to seize the historical sword. Consider Eldredge's cinematic example of what he envisions as a model father-son interaction: he fondly recalls the moment in the Kevin Costner movie *A Perfect World* in which the little boy pulls out his penis and Costner's character officially approves of its size. Eldredge writes, "A smile breaks out on [the boy's] face, like the sun coming up, and you know a major threshold has been crossed for him" (65-6). It certainly has. And yet, the journey across that threshold has been documented long before John Eldredge or even Kevin Costner. From cover to cover, Eldredge's book reads like nothing so much as a Freudian case study. In fact, behind the thinly veiled bravado that marches across the pages of *Wild at Heart* is a boy keening for a lost father—Eldredge even confesses that his own father was emotionally absent, a drunk who hid out in his garage (70-1).

Eldredge makes it all too easy to play analyst and grasp at his unapologetic symbolism of swords, penises, and even fathers as markers of a psychosexual development somehow stunted. But what should interest medievalists in such explicit connections among fathers, penises, and power is that they reveal the dark side of a desire for the 'dark ages.' Eldredge longs explicitly for the validation of his own patriarchal authority. Moreover, his attempt to find this validation in a fictional, hypermasculine Middle Ages is no isolated personal journey. The anxious medievalism of the American evangelical movement is the product of a desire to reinscribe a patriarchal authority that evangelicals perceive themselves as having lost—to reinstall it in their homes, their churches, and their schools by drawing meaning from what they envision as patriarchy's grand historical moment. The 'medieval' serves as that imagined space.

However, just because the evangelical desire for the Middle Ages is the desire for an imaginary, fictionalized, revised time and space does not mean that this movement has no legitimate ancestor to whom it can turn. Turn right, if you will, from Galahad Circle onto Rebel Drive, because this brand of neomedievalism is filtered through the lens of a medieval romance that America has had before. Though the historical knights that best exemplify the values, gender roles, and religious fervour desired by evangelicals today are hardly to be found in the medieval pages of Chrétien de Troyes or Thomas Malory, they *are* located in the Reconstruction fiction of southern preacher Thomas Dixon, specifically in the knightly incarnations of Dixon's own fantasy medievalism, the Knights of the Ku Klux Klan.[7]

Dixon's post-bellum "romance" *The Clansman* documents one of southern American masculinity's deepest traumas, the Civil War. The antebellum south had tried to justify slavery as a neofeudal regime, with plantation owners imagining themselves as medieval lords and ladies; but after he lost the Civil War, the southerner *really* got medieval, desperately longing for a source of power when his own masculinity had been severed.[8] What was the role of the white man, who had formerly held comprehensive power over other human beings, now that his rights would be shared by former slaves and, increasingly, even women? Moreover, what was the position of the southern man in America now that secession had failed? The south's anxious medievalism was, at its core, a blatant attempt to reinscribe hierarchies of gender and race. According to Morton W. Bloomfield, medievalism drew the southern imagination like flies to honey, providing the south with "'chivalric' modes of dominant masculinity and submissive femininity" (21). Languid ladies were redrawn as damsels in distress, lazy landowners reborn as crusading white knights. These portraits had intense social consequences. "Chivalry" came at a price for women, who had as little room for growth as they did to breathe in their corsets. Inevitably, feminine purity had to be protected, and African-American men suffered for decades under a gruesome plague of lynchings, murders committed by gangs of self-styled white knights who fancied themselves protectors of white womankind, much as anxious medievalism seeks to style its sons today.

Dixon's romance, in which white knights reclaim their broken manhood and the south by taking up the sword, is a convenient record of this rise of anxious medievalism in the Reconstruction era.[9] The novel traces a series of wounds to the southern white male's fragile masculinity: former slaves take over the government, the banks, and even the police force. The last straw is when a group of former slaves rape the innocent, virginal white Marion.[10] Once this final dominion of the white patriarchy has been breached, southern white men turn to the Middle Ages for redemption. The Klan members style themselves as reincarnated Scottish knights, and their uniforms are both medieval *and* phallic. Moonlight shimmers on their eighteen-inch tall caps, which are peaked into a "single spike held erect by a twisted wire" (315). The narrator even compares them to the "Knights of the Middle Ages [as they] rode on their Holy Crusades" (316). Dixon thus romanticizes the Klan's violence as chivalrous service to women. His knights claim to organize because, in their words, "In a land of light and beauty and love our women are prisoners of danger and fear" (319). Yet the novel's longing for racial hierarchy is exceeded only by its fear of the feminine. The villain of *The Clansman*, Austin Stoneman, turns out merely to have fallen prey to a controlling mulatto woman who has stolen so much power that she runs Senate proceedings and almost gets him to commit the ultimate sin against the patriarchy: the murder of his own son. Dixon's heroine, Elsie, is granted a dubious feminist statement early in the novel, lambasting her lover with the comically earnest pronouncement, "I deny your heaven-born male kingship," and declaring that she has no desire to be taken care of, "absorbed by a mere man" (127). Elsie is shown the error of her ways through the rape of Marion, who, significantly, is the only girl in the story who has no father to protect her. Elsie runs to her lover's side after the violent crime, declaring her former, feminist self "a vain, self-willed, pert little thing" (333). Elsie's submission, forced or chosen, is required for the Klan's triumphant rise, thanks to which "a gale of chivalrous passion…contagious and intoxicating, swept the white race" (341).

Anxious medievalism as a response to threatened masculinity seems to be equally as "contagious and intoxicating" in today's evangelical movement as it was in Dixon's Reconstruction south. It is possible, moreover, that both medievalist movements are responding to a deep, invasive, feminizing trauma. The wound to the masculinity of the nineteenth-century American south may correspond to a wounded Christian masculinity suffering from the shame of the terrorist attacks of September 11, 2001. America's terrorism-inspired masculinity crisis is the subject of a recent book by Susan Faludi, *The Terror Dream*. Faludi herself notes the connection between the 9/11 masculinity wound and the post-reconstruction American south, in which Klan attacks and lynchings served as a ceremony that "conferred a robe of knighthood on humiliated masculinity"(277). While studying the backlash against feminism inspired by the 2001 attack on the twin towers, she encounters "a disconcerting number" of voices claiming that the twin towers' collapse was a symbol of the nation's 'emasculation'"(9). By the estimate of popular media, the attacks caused "[a]n impotence that afflicted the nation at large" (53). According to Faludi, the answer to restoring our national erectile function was to be found in "cowboy culture," a mass reminiscence of the Wild West in which American men could imagine themselves as John Wayne, unapologetically masculine protectors of the fairer sex (4-5).[11]

For the evangelical movement, though, the Middle Ages seems to serve as an even more potent source of patriarchal justification.[12] And yet, Bruce Holsinger's recent study *Neomedievalism, Neoconservatism, and the War on Terror* asserts that neoconservatives repeatedly call the 9/11 terrorists "medieval" to make them seem like backwards demagogues. How do we reconcile that use of the term with the desire to re-enact the medieval on the part of the same voting block responsible for the aforementioned policies? The psychological bridge between the two may be found by returning to Stephen Ducat's *Wimp Factor*. Ducat points out that bigotry often results in "envy of that which one believes the despised other possesses" (70). The neoconservatives who describe the Middle East as "medieval" for its oppression of women and its barbaric masculinity were voted into power by members of the southern evangelical right, who seem to long for patriarchal supremacy, the very power that they attribute to their enemies. The desire of anxious medievalism is, at its core, a desire for the absolute patriarch in a world cleansed of the feminine, an all-powerful Alfather of a father, the manliest of men.

Except, those of us who remember that Julian of Norwich nursed at Jesus's breast, Christ was the manifestation of God's love, and Mary was the icon whose image all decent knights bore on their shields, know that this Alfather never existed. This fantasy of the fake Middle Ages is nothing more than the Law of the Father anxiously looking backwards for the legitimacy it never had: a distant phallus, distilled into dream vision.

WESLEYAN COLLEGE

NOTES

1   This paper was originally presented as "'Jesus Built My Hot-Rod': Masculinity, Medievalism, and the American Romance with God," at the 22nd International Conference on Medievalism, London, Ontario, Canada, October 2007.

2   For websites see Armor of God PJ's, LLC, http://www.armorofgodpjs.com; Rick Meyers, E-Sword Ministry, 2007, http://www.e-sword.net/; for books, see Shepherd, Lewis, and Wolfe.

3   See "The All-American *Boy's* Adventure Catalog." Here, one can also purchase a CD by Douglas Philips called *Rebuilding a Culture of Virtuous Boyhood*, the description of which distinctly fetishizes its medieval past: "Twenty-first century Christian boys have much to learn from boys of the past. Issues of courtesy to women, sacrifice, and vision are critical to raising modern boys. Our goal must be to move beyond the pretty platitudes and to aspire to rebuilding an entire culture of virtuous boyhood, such that every aspect of a young man's life is preparation for chivalrous leadership in the name of Jesus Christ." I was guided to this online catalogue by Sharlet 37.

4   The copyright for Lively's article states that it may be freely reproduced provided that contact information is provided. See the Works Cited for this information.

5   David, Moses, and other medievalized action figures can be found at www.christianbook.com

6   Specifically, Aronstein reads the politics of the Reagan era as "a dream of a 'true patriarchy' capable of restoring America to cultural and economic health" (146).

7   Kim Moreland and Susan Aronstein both locate the beginning of America's medieval romance in the nineteenth century, which, conveniently, is another time period in which America was embroiled in gender anxiety and issuing calls for a more masculine church. See Aronstein 2 and Moreland 1-5, who points out that this particular dream of the Middle Ages provided roots and stability in a time of chaos. Ducat points out that in the nineteenth century, "many religious authorities sought to erase the image of Jesus as a turn-the-other-cheek pacifist wuss" (62).

8   Barbara Ladd explains that "the southern states, economically dependent on slavery, opted for the attempted recreation of a stable hierarchical order pattered to some extent on European models and which limited the claims of citizenship to white men" (12).

9   The medievalism in *The Clansman* even includes a lost and fallen king: Abraham Lincoln. Lincoln is constructed as both a chivalrous gentleman and, oddly enough, a southerner. He bows to women "with the deference of a knight" (74), he is described as having a "lion heart" (72), and he is actually *against* emancipation, stating proudly that "The American is a citizen king or nothing" (46). As the great uniter of America, Lincoln is also a mystic and unmistakably Arthurian figure, often in a dreamy reverie, bathed in supernatural light. He has prophetic dreams and is taken to quoting Tennyson (52). In other words, Dixon's medievalism is hardly secessionist. Instead, it longs (much like the Arthurian legend it pilfers) for a united land under Confederacy.

10   As a result, Dixon's poor Marion commits suicide by throwing herself off a cliff after she is raped, declaring before she dies, "My name will always be sweet and clean" (305).

11   Faludi also locates the American expansion westward as a site of its original trauma, as American men found themselves unable to protect 'their women' from Native American warriors, or, worse yet, found themselves rejected by the women they attempted to rescue, who sometimes preferred the culture and company of their captors (200-16).

12   After all, as Faludi points out, even the firefighters who rescued people from the burning towers were compared repeatedly to knights and "medieval warriors" (68).

WORKS CITED

The All-American Boy's Adventure Catalog. The Vision Forum, Inc. 9 May 2008. <http://www.visionforum.com/boysadventure>

Aronstein, Susan. *Hollywood Knights: Arthurian Cinema and the Politics of Nostalgia.* New York: Palgrave, 2005.

Bloomfield, Morton W. "Reflections of a Medievalist: America, Medievalism, and the Middle Ages." *Medievalism in American Culture: Papers of the Eighteenth Annual Conference of the Center for Medieval and Early Renaissance Studies.* Eds Bernard Rosenthal and Paul E. Szarmach. Medieval & Renaissance Texts & Studies Vol. 55. Center for Medieval and Early Renaissance Studies, SUNY Binghampton: 1989. 13-29.

Dixon, Thomas. *The Clansman: An Historical Romance of the Ku Klux Klan.* 1905. Lexington: University Press of Kentucky, 1970.

Ducat, Stephen J. *The Wimp Factor: Gender Gaps, Holy Wars, and the Politics of Anxious Masculinity.* Boston: Beacon Press, 2004.

Eco, Umberto. "Dreaming of the Middle Ages." *Travels in Hyper Reality.* Trans. William Weaver. San Diego, CA: Harcourt Brace, 1986. 61-72.

Eldredge, John. *Wild at Heart: Discovering the Secrets of a Man's Soul.* Nashville, TN: Thomas Nelson, 2001.

Faludi, Susan. *The Terror Dream: Fear and Fantasy in Post-9/11 America.* New York: Metropolitan Books, 2007.

Holsinger, Bruce. *Neomedievalism, Neoconservatism, and the War on Terror.* Chicago: Prickly Paradigm Press, 2007.

Ladd, Barbara. *Nationalism and the Color Line in George W. Cable, Mark Twain, and William Faulkner.* Baton Rouge, LA: Louisiana State UP, 1996.

Lewis, Robert. *Raising a Modern-Day Knight: A Father's Role in Guiding His Son to Authentic Manhood.* Colorado Springs, CO: Focus on the Family Publications, 1997.

Lively, Scott. Abiding Truth Ministries, 6060 Sunrise Vista Drive, Citrus Heights, CA 95610, (916) 676-1057, lively@abidingtruth. www.abidingtruth.com, 2001. Accessed at http://defendthefamily.com, September 2007.

Moreland, Kim. *The Medievalist Impulse in American Literature.* Charlottesville, VA: U of Virginia P, 1996.

Philips, Douglas W. *Rebuilding a Culture of Virtuous Boyhood.* CD. The Vision Forum, Inc., n.d. http://www.visionforum.com/boysadventure.

_____. *Sleeping Beauty and the Five Questions.* CD. The Vision Forum, Inc., n.d. http://www.visionforum.com/beautifulgirlhood/productdetail.aspx?productid=32301&categoryid=53.

Sanderson, Richard A. "Wounded Masculinity." *MenWeb.* 2001. 9 May 2008. <http://www.menweb.org/woundedmasc>

Sharlet, Jeff. "Through a Glass, Darkly: How the Christian Right is Reimagining U.S. History." *Harper's* 313.1879 (December 2006): 33-43.

Shepherd, Sheri Rose. *His Princess: Love Letters from Your King.* Sisters, OR: Multnomah Books, 2004.

Wolfe, Alan B. *Balancing the Sword: A Comprehensive Study Guide to Life's Manual.* Tampa, FL: Vision Forum, Inc., 2005.

Heofen rece swealg: Neomedievalism and Spectacle in Grendel: Transcendence of The Great Big Bad

K.A. Laity

The opera *Grendel*, with music by Elliot Goldenthal and libretto by Julie Taymor and J.D. McClatchy, initially made more headlines for its technical challenges than for its text. However, the lively adaptation of John Gardner's novel brought a vivid sense of spectacle to his contemplative anti-war tale. While the librettists reproduced Gardner's disenchantment with war for a new (and perhaps equally disillusioned) audience, they also brought a new realization to the epic catastrophe of war, where its weight becomes literalized on stage by the central image of a giant, stony (but malleable) mountain wall. Grendel himself shatters into component selves as a child and as shadows, bringing to the physical spectacle a tangible sense of the fractured personality of the creature who is and is not "human." Using motifs of repetition and multiplicity, Taymor and McClatchy reinvent Gardner's own reimagining of the medieval heroic tale by complicating the narrative voice even as they simplify the overall narrative. Grendel's fractured narrative ends up as fragmented as the body parts of the men he destroys in an attempt to shape his narrative unity. Their bodies litter the strobe-lit stage in a spectacle of dissolution. Unable to find narrative coherence, Grendel's final act of self-annihilation comes not only as a relief, but as a triumph of narrative control: all the Grendels become one. Gardner found in the Danish court of the early Middle Ages a sinister clarity no longer possible—nor desirable—in American life. *Grendel* adds to this picture of the past a classical sort of beauty (best personified by the dancer who portrays Beowulf), but one that is ultimately trumped by the transcendent, if stark, beauty of the monster.

In their *Playbill* program for the Lincoln Center performances of the opera, co-librettist J.D. McClatchy writes of the medieval source tale: "the dark, ruthless grandeur of *Beowulf* stands literally at the forefront of English literature. The struggle it dramatizes, between the forces of light and dark, between a hero who arrives from a strange land and a monster that lurks at the bottom of our dreams, is a classic tale" (23). John Gardner's novel deliberately muddies the water of moral clarity the epic poem is generally believed to depict. Of course, any extended study of the poem complicates that picture, as the last century or so of Beowulf scholarship readily demonstrates. However, while the poem offers a few suggestions of apparent moral clarity ("that was a good king" or "as it is proper one should praise his lord with words"), the 1971 novel displaces a simplistic moral centre in favor of questions, trials and disputation. In the words of the director, "both subhuman and superhuman, bestial and divine, Grendel mirrors modern man, completely self-conscious, trapped in his own history, seeking the possibilities of optimism and redemption" (23). Clearly the creators' link is directly to Gardner's novel and not to its source text, a point Allan J. Frantzen makes repeatedly in his rather heated review of the opera in the *Old English Newsletter*. Rather than see this as a criticism, however, I'd like to explore what it means in terms of medievalism.

Behind Frantzen's review of the opera (which for the most part the Chicago Opera supporter scorned) is his dislike of Gardner's novel, in which he sees "numerous, often tedious idiosyncrasies" (31). Among these are the metaphorical connections to the signs of the zodiac (one can't help thinking that a medieval writer like Chaucer would differ on that point), which, repeated in the opera, he believes lead to "both excessive length and maximum incoherence" (31). He attributes the shock phrase "[t]his whole shit-ass scene was his idea, not mine" to the librettists, while it was in fact one of the many reversals of register appearing in Gardner's novel (31). The novel leaps nimbly between high and low, modern and medieval, human and mechanical throughout its course. As does the character of Grendel himself, it undergoes changes that touch on and spring away from the narrative of *Beowulf*. Like Stoppard's hapless characters in *Rosencrantz and Guildenstern are Dead*, Gardner's Grendel is sometimes aware of being part of a larger tale he cannot quite grasp, with its intimations of heroism, progress and material success that seem hollow lies to the marginalized monster.

It is this lost creature that the librettists appropriate. The rigid line between modern uncertainty and medieval clarity also survives the transition, and in fact the two draw apart. The medieval in their vision appears most clearly in the language. While Gardner's novel elicits the reader's sympathy using first-person narrative, the device works less clearly in the opera format. While the cynical play-by-play remains—amply supported by the amazing vocal work of Eric Owen—the visual spectacle crowds our eyes with dissenting information. In the novel we only hear Grendel's voice whispering or shouting in our ears, but onstage we see Grendel in his monstrous glory. Humanoid but never human, Grendel is also often accompanied by either his shadow selves or his mute and even more alien mother, or the rest of the shadowy Grendelkin. In Gardner's narrative we can be fooled by the humanity of the voice and forget the monstrous shape until our bond has been shaped and smoothed by familiarity.

In the opera, this identification occurs via language.[1] In a nod to the ultimate source text, the Danes speak Old English. This is not a choice for purists—should not the Danes speak Danish, the Geats some version of Swedish?—but a well-meaning gesture to credit the source text. (It is a more direct acknowledgement, as Frantzen notes, than that to scholars Roberta Frank and Eric Jager who helped create the Old English texts, but who appear only in the production staff credits of the program, sandwiched between the backstage conductors and diction coach.) However, this language choice also speaks to the story's place as a part of English speakers' past and language. It may indeed be a story of Scandinavian warriors, but it was recorded in English for whatever (disputed) variety of reasons, and looms spectre-like over the host of English masterpieces (or so my students seem to think). Goldenthal is conscious of the effect of weaving the Old English of the poem between

Gardner's modern English, commenting that, "Most of the main characters and the chorus are firmly planted in Anglo-Saxon or Old English soil. Only Grendel speaks our language" (24).

The use of Old English by the chorus and the human characters immediately contextualizes the scene for the audience. We first hear the alliterative cadences of the ancient tongue in a stately funeral scene with lines borrowed from the end of the poem:

> *Him tha gegiredan   Geata leode*
> *ad on eorthan   unwaclicne*
> *Har hilde rinc to Hronesnaesse*
> The tribesmen fashioned a funeral for their hero
> Stacking the logs up, a splendid tribute,
> And laid the great prince on the towering pyre.
>   (Taymor and McClatchy 5)

The chorus ends with the timeless words of enigmatic sorrow, *heofen rece swealg*, "heaven swallowed the smoke." The scene neatly accomplishes several things at once. Few will notice the very loose translation of the words, or that the end of the poem has been grafted onto the start of the opera. For most of the audience, this sequence instead offers a whiff of authenticity in the smoke. While the monstrous Grendel and the rutting ram that open both the opera and the novel could be of any time, or are at least not noticeably of a specific era (although his mechanistically themed monologue loosely suggests some kind of modernity), the stately funeral and the torch bearers evoke the past. The language itself, recognisable perhaps to only a small portion of any audience, immediately distances the listeners from the characters singing, forcing most of them to read the supertitles and evoking the distancing formality of ritual. Further, the scene and the language make clear that we are plunged into the past with all its suggestions of difference. We hover somewhere between Eco's models of the Middle Ages as pretext and the Middle Ages as ironic revisitation (Eco 68-9). While the Beowulf funeral scene clearly offers a pretext to situate the narrative, it is not as cavalier as many of the other uses to which Eco refers. While there is more than a generous helping of irony in the medievalism of the scene—and in the use of Old English throughout—I would argue that, rather than simply a naïve or parodic effect, the creators seek to establish a sense of deference to their source materials and a genuine discourse about its conventions (however naïve or parodic a discourse results).

For the librettists, the Middle Ages of the *Beowulf* narrative set a mark in human history—even more specifically, in the history of English speakers. Innocuously defined by Taymor as a ninth-century poem, *Beowulf* as appropriated in select lines of Old English poetry appears to present the unquestioning loyalty of the family for the fallen troops of war. In the present climate it is difficult not to draw the same anti-war parallels most readers drew from Gardner's novel, published in the midst of the Vietnam conflict, where the lone monster speaks against the military might of the fighters. The warrior chorus that begins Scene III combines the conservative appeal of the

Old English language with sloganeering sufficiently heated to suit any Fox
News broadcast:

> *Cringe hildlatan, tydre treowlogan* Crush the cowards, force is strong
> *Thrym sceal mid wlencu, iren ecg* Swords bring honor, never wrong
> *Fyr sceal faran, feage sweltan* Fire cleanses, life is cheap
> *Manna ealdian, meowle weopan.* Old men shiver, women weep. (11)

One cannot help thinking that the script-writers have located that past era that
many conservatives seem to long for when referring to a lost time of moral clarity
and military values. To put it in other terms, we could see a parallel with Arthur
Lindley's cinematic reworking of Eco's little Middle Ages. Although Lindley
writes specifically about film, we can see the same sort of visual shorthand at
work on the stage. Lindley describes his fourth version of the era as:

> The Middle Ages as a game preserve—or elephant's graveyard—for
> unironized heroism, the purpose it was also serving when transposed
> into that extended and conscious tribute to Joseph Campbell, *Star
> Wars* (USA 1977), and continues to serve with conspicuous commercial
> success in *Braveheart*. Like the preceding categories, this is also an
> example of the use of the Middle Ages as a mode of psychological
> and social simplification: a distancing device, like the bark-paintings
> which provide visual models for the style of *The seventh seal*, meant
> to show us the rude outline of things.

This simplicity of thought is what the librettists, Gardner and their Grendels
fight against, interrogating the binaries of a world where "you're with us or
you're against us," to borrow a phrase.

This is nowhere more clearly demonstrated than in the character of the
Shaper, whose discourse is allowed to span both the modern and medieval
versions of English. He enters the story with a song approximating the opening
lines of the poem:

> Oft Scyld Shefing Gar-Dena folctoga
> In geardagum maertha gewann
> Morth-sceathan cwealda, meodo-aern geblodgode
> *Meowlum heofungdagas, maewas maenende.*
> Oft Scyld Shefing, the Speardanes' swift lord,
> In days long gone, gained great glory,
> Murdered marauders, their meadhalls gory,
> Their women dragged to woe, wailing seabirds. (14)

In the poem, this is the point at which we meet Grendel. As Jeffrey Jerome
Cohen has written on the epic,

> Grendel's relation to the *comitatus* of Heorot is one of illustrative
> antithesis... Grendel represents a cultural Other for whom conformity
> to societal dictates is an impossibility because those dictates are not
> comprehensible to him; he is at the same time a monsterized version
> of what a member of that very society can become when those dictates
> are rejected, when the authority of leaders or mores disintegrates and
> the subordination of the individual to hierarchy is lost. (26)

Gardner's book and the opera, however, present us with the monster's view from the start, depicting the homogenous and artificially constructed world of the Danes as an attractive illusion that appears to offer reconciliation to the monster. Initially, Grendel and his shadows are united by the song of the shaper: the history of the Danes, which is a lie, but a convincing lie. Previously, the shadows had repeated their source at intervals like imperfect echoes. Here, however, they all sing in unison:

> The sheer sound of it!
> Even to me it made
> Glorious sense. (14)

On stage, the shaper's work is made literal by light creating "images of glory," including "shining armored heroes, a royal wedding couple, etc." and eventually the meadhall, Heorot (14). The shaper's words reach Grendel before translation, reaching the audience both through the supertitles and through the modern version, sung as the images project on the backdrop when the song turns to praising Hrothgar. The shaper is the bridge between the medieval past and the modern present, just as he is the bridge between the human warriors and the monstrous Other. In Gardner's novel, the shaper has a similar effect, although we do not hear his verses, but only see them on the page (replicating more directly the opening lines of the poem). We see the effect on Grendel, first as he contemplates the ragtag bunch of killers transformed into a group of shining warriors, musing "Well then, he's changed them…why not?" He becomes infected by the "pompous," "the projected possible" (48-9). In performance, this eruption presents to the audience the power of the past as well as that of the shaper, implying that this sacred past can transform the cynical present, make it amenable to those high ideals—if only for a brief time. As Grendel and his three shadows connect and repeat their dialogue, the opportunity exists for concord. The opportunity is, of course, rife with irony as well, with the monster and his three shadows singing together the lines, "Daylong, nightlong, torn apart, torn apart by song" (16). They howl like beasts as they approach most closely the human moment, perhaps because there is no discourse for the cursed.

However, the moment quickly passes, and Grendel must return from medieval unity to modern fracture. Sure enough, the naming of the enemy and the exposing of his lineage accomplishes the deed. "The murderous sinful spirit" who is "spawn of the dark side, the ever-damnèd race of Cain" reacts with alarm to this naming, this location in a specific tradition, even as he sings in unison with the shaper, co-creating this identity. Grendel has understood the lies of the shaper even as he gave in to their seduction, but now he accepts at face value the powerful words of blame and accusation, because he has wanted to be part of the distant, ideal world of the medieval harper and the illusion he spins for the warriors and the audience. Because the shaper sings in Modern English, Grendel has been able to understand him, even joining him harmoniously on the repeated lines which identify him by name and tie him to Cain, as if they were creating his identity jointly in the final act of congruence that Grendel can achieve with the shaper's discourse. The break occurs when Grendel takes the lead, singing alone, immediately followed by the chorus' return to Old English, translating his words and separating him once more from the medieval discourse, *Se myrthu, blodgeotende synscatha Grendel* (17).

For a moment Grendel and his shadows forge their final unity, crying "Mercy" and "Peace" in unison, but immediately thereafter his own speech breaks down in the face of the warriors' rejection and subsequent attack, literally attempting to dissociate the parts of Grendel. His fractured speech mirrors this dissolution:

I... I've been...
They hurt... they hurt me.
Venom...
They hurt me. Venom...
They want to kill me.
They could kill me. (17)

His shadows pick up this thread, but rather than unity we once again have the disruptive sound of off-beat repetition, the same phrases at different intervals, repeating, overlapping, losing coherence. While Grendel tries to hold onto the medieval ideal, he struggles for control of the discourse with his own shadows, with the warriors, and even with the shaper. His anger and disillusionment coalesce around the fervid pronouncement, "Bullshit!"

This is Grendel's waking moment in the opera, as if the lure of the uncomplicated past has finally roused him from a dream. It also signals the very postmodern appearance of the dragon, rendered in the opera by a multiplicity of voices—like Grendel himself—and by a gendering that shifts our reading of the character from that presented in Gardner's novel. Mezzo-soprano Denyce Graves offers a slinky personification of the character who cannot possibly have the same effect on the opera's audience as the original does upon Grendel (or perhaps, we can guess, the creators and presenters would not wish to have their audience frightened enough to have to worry, as Grendel does, about retaining bowel control). Paralleling Grendel's dissolution into fractured selves—surely the marker of the modern within the opera—the dragon also has three dragonettes; however, they do not highlight fragmentation so much as they emphasize the dragon's dominant personality, although even in the novel he greets his fellow monster with the words, "We've been expecting you" (58). Gardner's dragon, though, has the voice of an old man, which Grendel finds "startling" (58). The composer, Goldenthal, confesses that one of the biggest challenges of the score was "creating a voice for the Dragon. My first impulse was to eliminate gender, so I arrived at the concept of a 'baritone-soprano.' A female singing fortissimo in an unexpected male range is a very disconcerting and threatening sound" (23). While the female appearance of the singers undercuts that removal of gender-specificity, the audience—comprised of modern, fractured selves—grasps the attempt to dislocate both voice and gender.

Gardner's dragon claims to "know everything...the beginning, the present, the end. Everything. You now, you see the past and the present, like other low creatures ...but dragons, my boy, have a whole different kind of mind" (62-3). The dragon can see the same elusive past that Grendel longs for in the warriors' meadhall, but he can also see the future the *Beowulf*-poet imagines too: the meadhall in ruins, destroyed by fire. The dragon is aware of the illusion the carefully crafted world of the shaper offers. This knowledge renders it as empty as the treasure hoard—nothing but habit in a meaningless world. Despite its possession of greater knowledge, the dragon is unable to forge any kind of satisfying response to this knowledge, which is what Grendel seeks. Eschewing any possible answer other than hoarding gold, the dragon finally offers Grendel purpose through a kind of Hegelian dialectic with his would-be friends—to be the Other who spurs them on to accomplishment, investing their notions of heroism (already cast by language into the archaic past) with a passing meaning, while acknowledging that it, like the more tangible treasures, will one day become dust. Yet the dragon meddles, charming the Grendelkin, as if to acknowledge our powerlessness before endless repetition. As Cohen says of monstrous *extimité*, "the past is always with us, active and engaged, as dangerous as it is enticing, as violent as it is compelling, as unassimilable as it is familiar" (186). The modern audience may lack the dragon's omniscient sight and memory, but it can appreciate the monster within more readily, perhaps, than the medieval audience could, and can share a vicarious thrill.

We can trace the passage of Grendel's fragmentation, from his claws and jaws to the dismembered bodies of his victims in the meadhall. In perhaps the most stunning moment of the entire opera, enacted with puppetry and lighting effects, the slaughter pins spectacle to bloodshed and asks the audience to witness the carnage which the stage directions describe as "the 'strobe' slaughter," where "flashes of human bodies in contorted positions are caught as they fly through the air. Close-ups of fragmented faces and body parts, and shattered pieces of furniture. Flashes of Grendel's maniacal face appear, filling the space" (29). The awe of spectacle removes us from sympathy for the murdered Danes. The use of the puppetry, far from infantilizing, as Frantzen claims (32), offers the engaged viewer the ability nimbly to shift from the humanity of Grendel as played by Owens, to the monstrous giant who overwhelms the mead hall. The artifice removes the audience members from their own monstrosity as they thrill to the sensory barrage. As Cohen has said, "Because he conjoins enjoyment and prohibition in culturally transformable ways, because he seems fully exterior to masculine self-identity at the same time as he performs his identity-giving work at the heart of embodied subjectivity, the giant returns" (186). The monster Grendel allows a temporary transcendence of the merely human, a thrill-ride through the monstrous sufficiency which he proclaims to be "huge as horror. Hard as bone. I am Me! At last! At last I am alone!" (30). The act ends, with a blackout, at these gloating words.

Choked with smugness at his new invulnerability, Grendel inhabits his monstrous skin more easily, humiliating the would-be hero Unferth (as in the novel) with a hail of apples rather than the expected teeth and claws. Although he sings, "balance is everything," Grendel's gleeful dance shows that he has tipped over into monstrosity. The balance of audience sympathy has shifted toward the human. Unferth, who despite his initial humiliation enters Grendel's cave announcing "*Unferth is cumen*," eventually transforms from a medieval hero to a postmodern anti-hero, demanding in modern English, "No, listen! No, listen!" even as he dismisses "words [as] clouds" (33-34). Grendel is left repeating, "that word, 'hero,' is beginning to grate" (35). It seems entirely fitting that it is the shadow Grendels who finally drag the hero from the cave back to safety. While Grendel muses on his own weakness ("If I murdered Hrothgar and all the Scyldings, what would I live for?"), he returns to some semblance of humanity and community.

As Cohen has noted, the monstrous has a problematic gendering, particularly if we align the monstrous Grendel with his giant nature: while "the giant is encountered in the performance of a masculinity as necessary as it is obscene," it is also the case that "the giant shares more with the feminine, and specifically with the maternal, than his excessively male form might suggest" (xii). Grendel's mother—a tree-like figure of even greater alterity than her son in this production—often shadows her monstrously giant offspring, alternately restraining or being restrained by him. The silence and problematic nature of the monstrous female body prepares us for a tantalizing view of the human female body, which offers a hope of unity to Grendel. The idea of the queen arrives with the entourage of Wealtheow, as if she were a Britney or a Lindsay for public consumption—her reality as unknown to the men in the meadhall as to the monster who dreams of final union through her. To emphasize the creativity inherent in the female flesh, "Wealtheow's hair, stretched out, becomes a giant harp upon which her attendants play" (36). She has the power to transform not only the failing heroes of the meadhall and Hrothgar himself, but the monster, too. Wealtheow reshapes the world once more. As a contemplative Grendel sings,

> The old king is moved, as if by the Shaper's song,
> Not visions of a glorious past,
> But of present beauty,
> A beauty that stops time's flow... (37).

Grendel keeps up a façade of unrepentant monstrosity, dismissing the lovers as "slime to slime" and "ashes to ashes," but the shadow Grendels sing the queen's praises. Goldenthall himself notes that "Wealtheow embodies pure, present beauty. Her voice is celestial, possessing a shimmering, resonant humanity" (23). Confused by her approachable femininity, Grendel recedes into the embrace of his mother. In the following scene, where "a glass boat travels through the shimmering waves of moonlight," we see that the shadow Grendel—the most human part of him—may approach her, but his truest self remains aloof. In a song reminiscent of the enigmatic poem "Wulf and Eadwacer," Wealtheow and the shadow Grendel drift along singing, "*We sind ungelice* [We are something different]" and "*Mot ic the lufian* [Can I love you?]" (39). Yet when the shadow

Grendel reaches for her, he receives a rebuff: "she slaps him, and he falls off the boat, sinking downward, as Wealtheow swiftly floats away" (39). While the shadow self can approach the feminine ideal, the monster must be kept at arm's length. Even at the moment of destruction, Wealtheow, too, must be displaced: she is played by a doll to maintain the illusion of Grendel's relative size when, enraged by her refusal, the monster returns seeking vengeance. As the staggered lines sung by Wealtheow, Unferth and Hrothgar show, the hyper-masculine world of the meadhall has been splintered by her presence, too. While Grendel menaces the doll Wealtheow and vacillates between destruction and mercy, ultimately declaring any difference between the choices "meaningless" (40), he realizes that he is once more marginalized and separated not only from the heroes, but also from himself; he is "a creature of two minds" (41), one human, one monstrous. This outcome seems to fulfill Taymor's claimed intention: "Both subhuman and superhuman, bestial and divine, Grendel mirrors modern man, completely self-conscious, trapped in his own history, seeking the possibilities of optimism and redemption" (25). There are no easy answers for the monster, but his final encounter with heroic ideals has yet to come.

Beowulf, in Gardner's novel, is mechanistic and menacing. In the opera, we cannot be certain that the boy-harper who picks up the late shaper's harp has not created him in the process of recounting the hero's departure for Denmark. Grendel's ascension to the top of the malleable mountain seems to suggest that word has led to deed, as he sings of the joy he feels for "a whole new game" (43). In the novel, the mechanistic Geats clank into the hall, led by the beardless, insane leader, "his mind working, stone-cold, grinding like a mill wheel" (161). For the opera, the producers cast dancer Desmond Richardson. While his ballet retains that precision and flawless exactitude, the hard body of the hero contrasts with the softness of his fluid movements and the vulnerability of the visible flesh of the stripped-down dancer. Gardner's hero retains the menace of the dragon, his hand closing "like a dragon's jaw" on Grendel's, while he sprouts "fiery wings" and "flames slip out at the corners of his mouth" (168-70). He unites Grendel with the knowledge of his finitude, forcing the monster to acknowledge the truth with his own song. In the opera, however, Grendel has been given voice all along, so the reversal comes through Beowulf's silence (the chorus sings for him, as if in tacit approval) and through his mobility. While Grendel once gives us a caricature of dance to show his gleefulness, he relies primarily on voice, rather than movement, throughout the performance. As the whimpering Grendel perches on the cliff edge in the novel, "quaking with fear" he looks into "bottomless blackness," which is "moving [him] slowly to [his] voluntary tumble into death" (173). The librettists shift the focus of this final scene slightly, allowing the monster to claim the darkness, depths and death; he is not "some monster" looking into watery depths, but says, "there is a monster inside me, deep inside, a deep-sea wonder" (46). Taymor and McClatchy retain the implication of voluntary action toward death, but displace it to the monster consciousness, "a monster in [Grendel] moving [him] to fall" (47). While Gardner's monster dies with "evil, incredibly stupid" creatures looking on, Grendel and his shadows in the opera claim volition before the human audience, echoed by the chorus which proclaims, "I will fall. I want to fall. I will my fall" (47)—rendering much more enigmatic the final mixture of joy and desire that we may all share the experience of Grendel's accident. While Gardner's anti-hero emphasizes the random nature of life, the opera's Grendel offers a chance to recognize and embrace the monstrous under our own skins. The opera's Beowulf is not the mechanistic monster of the novel, but a human playing a heroic role; we can see the ideal, yet we admire the very real body achieved by discipline and ambition. As McClatchy writes in the program notes,

We hope this opera will upend conventional categories. We hope it is simultaneously funny and menacing. We hope it both dazzles and clarifies, delights and instructs. We hope you take this monster home with you. He's for your dreams and for your conscience. We hope he haunts them both. (26)

While we may not reach the perfection of the hero, our only other option need not be becoming the monster. If we fall from the heights, we need not sink to the depths.

While I hope that some of my thoughts have survived the transmission of writing a memory, I am ever more acutely aware of trying to dissect an ephemeral puff of smoke—a performance—from the fractured remnants it leaves behind: a program, a libretto, a handful of reviews and news stories. Yet again *heofen rece swealg* and I am left uncertain whether what I experienced in the Lincoln Center in July 2006 approaches in any way the "text" (in its most slippery modern sense) that I attempt to pin down in this essay, but there is an exhilaration in attempting to capture something so elusive. Just as the shaper's song gives way to the boy-harper's melody, old stories dance to new tunes, providing transition without interruption. I would agree with Lisi Oliver that "it is a triumph for medievalism that a major opera company was willing to invest such a considerable amount of money on a new production based, at least indirectly, on *Beowulf*" (22), but I find it more of a triumph that old monsters find new audiences and tale tellers, even if they might fail to live up to some scholars' notions of "authenticity." "Is it joy I feel?" Or just the "monster in me moving me to fall"? In becoming an opera, perhaps Grendel's had an accident, but in the nicest way possible, let me echo him—"so may you all"—for in our accidental discoveries lie the greatest treasures of all. Our monsters will always rise, both appealing to us and frightening us. To survive, we need to find ways to let the monsters within sing in harmony with our human voices.

COLLEGE OF SAINT ROSE

NOTES

1 I am grateful to Gary Murphy, Director of Public Relations at the Los Angeles Opera, for access to a copy of the libretto script.

WORKS CITED

Cohen, Jeffrey Jerome. *Of Giants: Sex, Monsters and the Middle Ages.* Medieval Cultures 17. Minneapolis: U of Minnesota P, 1999.

Eco, Umberto. "Dreaming of the Middle Ages." *Travels in Hyperreality.* New York: Harcourt Brace, 1986. 61-72.

Frantzen, Allen J. "'Hrothgar Built Roads': *Grendel*'s Ride in LA." *Old English Newsletter* 39.3 (2006): 27-35.

Gardner, John. *Grendel.*1971. New York: Vintage, 1989.

Grendel: Transcendence of The Great Big Bad: An Opera. Music by Elliott Goldenthal. Libretto by Julie Taymor and J.D. McClatchy. Unpublished script, 2006.

Grendel: Transcendence of The Great Big Bad. Music by Elliott Goldenthal. Libretto by Julie Taymor and J.D. McClatchy. Dir. Julie Taymor. Perf. Eric Owens, Richard Croft, Denyce Graves, Desmond Richardson, et al. Lincoln Center, New York. 13 July 2006.

"Grendel: Transcendence of The Great Big Bad." *Playbill: Lincoln Center Festival 2006.* 19-45.

"Individual Contributors." *Chicago Opera Theater.* 31 Aug 2007. 13 October 2007. <http://www.chicagooperatheater.org/support/individual_contributors.html>

Lindley, Arthur. "The ahistoricism of Medieval Film." *Screening the Past* 3 (29 May 1998). 13 May 2008. <http://www.latrobe.edu.au/screeningthepast/firstrelease/fir598/ALfr3a.htm>

Lunden, Jeff. "*Grendel*: An Operatic Monster's Tale." *All Things Considered.* 11 July 2006. National Public Radio. 13 October 2007. <http://www.npr.org/templates/story/story.php?storyId=5542123>

Oliver, Lisi. "A Banner Year for *Beowulf* on the Boards." *Old English Newsletter* 39.3 (2006): 22-26.

Last Speakers of Occitan and the Medieval Past: A Summer Festival

Catherine Parayre

Very few readers and critics are aware that contemporary Occitan literature produces works of high quality.[1] In fact, it is usually considered that twelfth-century troubadour lyric forms an unsurpassed corpus in that language. In the present study however, I will examine a contemporary cultural event in which reference to the Occitan medieval past may be interpreted as a troubled sign, rather than as one more illustration of the belief that it constitutes the best of what Occitan has ever offered. Looking at a summer festival, *L'Estivada,* which the city of Rodez in the south of France has organized since 1995, I will argue that the rationale of this one-week event celebrating Occitan culture not only reduces the world and words of the troubadours to an oversimplified image, but also, and more importantly, establishes them as symbols of a dramatic cultural crisis. In other words, I want to look at the ways in which the very beginnings of Occitan literature may also evoke its end.

L'Estivada attracts visitors from across the country. The numbers are telling: from about two to three thousand visitors in 1996 festival attendance grew to more than forty thousand in 2006.[2] Such statistics are remarkable and, indeed, the success of *L'Estivada* needs to be emphasized. Rodez, with its 27,000 inhabitants, is of little interest to tourists by comparison with other cities in the south of France. Yet, in a region where tourism plays a major economic role[3] and where occasions for entertainment are in no way lacking, the city has found a cultural niche with this festival. Typically, the program of *L'Estivada* features music as well as theater performances, film screenings, storytelling, and literary cafés. Although a few of these events (for instance, recitations of troubadour songs) focus on the Occitan medieval past, the festival aims at an audience well aware of contemporary trends. This is particularly true of musical performances if one judges by some of the terms used: *groov'oc, blues r'occitan* or *rock occitan.* Several locations in the city host different spectacles. However, the central area is the "village" where, in addition to offering a stage for some of the events listed on the program, vendors sell arts and crafts as well as regional food specialties. Various regional publishing houses and associations promoting Occitan are also present at the festival "village." *L'Estivada* thus offers a dynamic picture of Occitan culture and language for one week, creating the impression that vibrant Occitan social and cultural structures exist today. During the festival, one frequently hears the Occitan language, an otherwise rare occurrence nowadays; the Occitan flag is everywhere to see; promoters of the language and of its literature are given exposure. Most of all, the festival attracts a diverse audience, in particular among the younger generation. Announced as a celebration of "Occitania," it is an anticipated summer highlight in the region.

Nevertheless, such effervescence and celebratory spirit cannot or should not hide the fact that the very existence of this festival and the reason why it is so successful derive directly from the dire circumstances of the Occitan language and of the culture in which it traditionally thrived. In fact–and although *L'Estivada* is, quite legitimately, the occasion for festivities during summer vacation and an unlikely place or time to wonder in depth about some of its ideological premises–the public is probably aware of the cultural tensions or malaise which the very objective of *L'Estivada* reveals. *L'Estivada* is thus no different from other similar events in which a minority culture is put on display: it is "a means of coping with social crisis" (Picard and Robinson 14).

For instance, the very use of the term "Occitania" on the festival website suggests a problematic discourse fostered by a difficult social environment. "Occitania" designates seven regions in France, as well as the Val d'Aran in Spain and a few alpine valleys in Italy, where Occitan was traditionally spoken, but the term remains contested. Some critics argue that it lacks historical accuracy and is used mostly to refer to a regional identity of which there is little trace in today's society; at the same time, it has been appropriated by a militant discourse desperately struggling to find widespread support and legitimacy.[4]

Similarly, the organizers of the 2006 edition of the festival invited Renaud de Donnedieu Vabres, then French Minister of Culture, to attend the festivities, a puzzling fact considering that France never ratified the 1992 European Charter for Regional and Minority Languages obligating European countries actively to protect such languages.[5] Indeed, over the centuries France has taken various measures to eradicate from its territory all languages other than French, these being dismissed, in a derogatory way, as mere *patois*. In fact, Ernest Renan claims in his celebrated essay "What is a Nation?" that French national unity was achieved only to the extent that large sections of the population were made to forget their regional past (166). This argument certainly applies to the Occitan past, so that it can be asked, perhaps cynically, why someone in the official position of de Donnedieu Vabres would extol Occitan culture and express admiration for its history.[6]

As for the Occitan language, there is no doubt that it is dying. The festival website claims that fifteen per cent of those under twenty-five years of age speak the language. Clearly inaccurate, this statistic greatly exceeds reality. Although the language can still be ehard, especially among the older generation, it is estimated that hardly any native speaker of Occitan was born after the 1960's (Kremnitz 244). The language is hardly taught and is of negligible significance in the economic sector; furthermore, the literature it still produces is little sold, little read and utterly ignored by the French cultural elites (Gardy 14-15). One might say that the festival celebrates Occitan when, in fact, there is little enough to celebrate. However successful it is, *L'Estivada* stages the dissolution of the very culture it puts on display. Assuredly, various elements within the festival, whether political speeches or the presence of associations defending the language, demonstrate clearly the current crisis in Occitan.

Most interestingly, the medieval theme, as it appears on the festival website and on its program, is also a symptom of this crisis. The fact that a long history of cultural repression followed the medieval period obviously explains why the festival program and its website give weight to medieval themes. Indeed, if no one today, except for a few specialists, can provide the name of a contemporary Occitan author, millions of individuals, not just in a university, will use or at least recognize the term *troubadour*. It is therefore not surprising that five out of the ten venues of the festival are given a name containing a medieval allusion. These are *jocs, trobar, convivencia, fin'amor*, and *paratge*.[7] The program is likewise organized around the same headings. In summer 2006, the website outlined a rationale for the presence of medieval references on the program and in the physical geography of the festival. These explanations, from the website, are: "Occitan civilization reached its peak in the twelfth century with the troubadours and is characterized by a natural ability to accept, among its own, the coexistence of multiple opinions and diverse groups."[8] Its values are:

> *Paratge*: true nobility of the heart and spirit. *Convivencia*: knowing how to live together as equals in the respect of difference. *Trobar*: the one who goes on a quest and innovates in the arts and poetry as well as is able to envision a better society. *Jovent*: spirit of modernity in the younger generations. *Fin'amor*: idea of refinement, mystical ecstasy. *Joi*: state of exaltation, inner transport comparable to the *duende* (Spain) or the *tarab* (Arabic). As one may see, these six words are enough to evoke a civilization…[9]

A few lines down, the troubadours are again mentioned as best representing these values. These definitions are accompanied by a brief summary of Occitan history, in which one can read statements about the medieval period such as: "Human contacts became such that all found a new self in this essentially civilizing climate and felt that they could bring to the world an extraordinary concept of humanity: '*Fin'amor*'… This civilization is based on the notion of '*Paratge*,' which represents equality in its state of nature." This oversimplified and highly essentialist account of medieval history and of the role of the troubadours is, of course, a nostalgic one which does not fail to remind us of the precarious situation characterizing Occitan today.

If one believes critics such as Abdul JanMohamed and David Lloyd, such formulations are typical of minority discourse, which they describe as being "the product of damage–damage more or less systematically inflicted on cultures produced as minorities by the dominant culture" (4). They continue: "The pathos of hegemony is frequently matched by its interested celebration of differences, but only of differences in the aestheticized form of recreations. Detached from the site of their production, minority cultural forms become palatable" (5). The Occitan medieval past is thus perceived, without any reservation whatsoever, as a superior cultural model to emulate and the origin of the most admirable values. One might add that, within the context of the festival, such a celebration of the Occitan medieval past does not represent any challenge to or questioning of the dominant group, namely French institutions and culture, since this discourse remains confined to the arena of entertainment.

Clearly, *L'Estivada* is not designed to articulate or achieve the means to effect radical change.

Two major aspects of the festival, both reinforced by reference to the medieval world, convey this impression that no radical change will ever be possible for Occitan. The first deals more with form than with content. Reduced to a few catchphrases, the medieval theme structures the presentation of *L'Estivada* and appears to be no more than an organizing principle patching up the cultural collage constituted by the various activities and events on the program. In the words of Umberto Eco in his study on how we perceive the Middle Ages today, the medieval past is in this case a *pretext* ("Dreaming" 68). In the case of *L'Estivada*, recuperating the Middle Ages serves a purpose both ideological (Occitan is thus presented as being something other than just a *patois*; like French, it has a long tradition and rich literature) and economic (to attract tourists, the festival, like all such events, needs to be neatly packaged). In "A Theory of Expositions," Eco contends that "[i]n contemporary expositions a country no longer says 'Look what I produce' but 'Look how smart I am in presenting what I produce'"(296).[10] In other words, "in an exposition we show not the objects but the exposition itself. The basic ideology of an exposition is that the packaging is more important than the product" (299). This argument finds a broad echo in postmodern societies; indeed, in our photographic and multimedia age, packaging is key to every aspect of life (Sontag 3-4). It is therefore commonly accepted that identity, individual and cultural, is a fluid construct. Celia Lury suggests: "The collage displaces the narrative as the privileged technique of self" (84). We have become "experimental individuals" eager to "reconstitute" our individuality "as a set of [flexible] cultural or stylistic resources" (85, 23).

This is indeed what happens at the festival in Rodez: elements of Occitan culture are collected, assembled, adapted and estheticized to ensure that visitors will enjoy the show and that the event will be a financial success. By bringing cultural elements together and displaying them for the world to see (including on the internet), such an event creates, at least for a short while, a sense of community otherwise illusory and 'elusive,' to use a term from Zygmunt Bauman on similar issues (1). Picard and Robinson write:

> Both the tourist and festival goer are engaged in transformative events
> where the notion of re-enchantment does not only refer to the process
> of structural repair or return to a communal feeling of primordial
> delight, but also to the individual's (re)introduction to a magical time
> where all things appear possible (17).

During *L'Estivada*, the medieval period functions as a simulacrum to be filled with the organizers' and spectators' expectations and wishes. It is therefore tempting, and in fact partially accurate, to say that *L'Estivada* is instrumental in the attempt to create a new Occitan self, one attuned to contemporary lifestyles and aesthetic concerns. However, this positive reading is true only to a limited extent, not only because *L'Estivada* is the exhibition of a dying culture, but also because, as Eco argues, it is simply an exhibition: "[e]xhibitions assume the form of an inventory...They seem to be a final recapitulation in the face of a hypothetical end of the world" ("Theory" 292).

In fact, the other way in which the use of the medieval during *L'Estivada* reinforces the impression that our century will see the end of Occitan is the reference to a common topos in modern and recent Occitan literature, namely the theme of the last speaker of the language. In particular, the emphasis put on medieval literature and culture coincides with the omission on the program of other Occitan literary periods and movements. These include the Félibrige movement in the nineteenth century whose central figure, Frédéric Mistral, was awarded the Nobel prize for literature, and, by the middle of the twentieth century, a new generation of writers, among them Jean Boudou, Robert Lafont, and Bernard Manciet, whose works have captured the interest, if not of the masses, at least of various critics around the world. This omission may appear somewhat curious if one considers that the members of the Félibrige were keen on exhibiting southern and Provençal culture and organized numerous meetings where good food, literary readings and entertaining spectacles attracted visitors just as *L'Estivada* does.[11] One major difference, however, applies: the Félibrige was adamantly militant; *L'Estivada* is more about fun. The Félibrige wanted to motivate; *L'Estivada* wants to amuse. Still, both Félibrige events and *L'Estivada* have one crucial point in common: they thematize the death of the language. The Félibrige does so directly, both in militant speeches and in its literature, among whose major themes is the disappearance of the last witness to southern culture. One generation later, this theme of the last speaker or witness will be found repeatedly in Occitan literature, in particular in the works of Lafont and Boudou, which poignantly retrace the existential misery of the individual who has no one left to speak to because no one understands him and who, by the same token, is tragically aware that the remnants of an entire culture will disappear with him.

The website of *L'Estivada* conveys, albeit implicitly, a similar message by bringing up the medieval past and ignoring more recent Occitan texts, as if to say that the troubadours were the last true speakers of a language doomed to oblivion. In other words, the medieval past seems to mark the end of Occitan history. The medieval reference on the website and on the program of *L'Estivada* should therefore be interpreted not just as a neat extra touch, but also as one more component in the problematic of the last speaker. At the festival in Rodez, the evocation of the Middle Ages clearly claims an Occitan identity which remains, for the most part, a lost identity. As is the case with other regional festivals, the entertainment hides and denies the death, or impending death, of what it celebrates. During *L'Estivada*, the last speaker, by whom this death is announced, is a medieval speaker.

BROCK UNIVERSITY

NOTES

1 For instance, William Calin writes: "The present situation–going back a number of decades–offers the paradox of literature flourishing at its greatest as the language itself is in the process of dying or, at least, is at its nadir. This means that more and better writers write while fewer people (including readers) speak, and therefore that as the writers find themselves severed from the living dialect base of the language, they have to rely upon the high-culture tongue–synthetic, plastic, chemical–of their own making, and can also rely upon and incorporate all of world literature available to them" (320).

2 All references to *L'Estivada* are taken from the festival website, http://www.estivada-rodez.com/acceil.php, consulted over the spring and summer 2007 until early September 2007. Over this period of time, the site included statistics on and information about the 2006 edition as well as the program for the 2007 edition. The site is continually updated. Statistics on festival attendance were listed in the section "Historique." All translations from the website are my own.

3 See, for instance, http://www.tourisme.gouv.fr.

4 For instance, Philippe Gardy considers that the term "Occitania" evokes "an a-historical essentialism." Gardy contends that there exists indeed an Occitan "space," the "product" of a long historical and cultural evolution, but that there has never been any clear conception of an Occitan "territory" (153-4).

5 Thirty-three European countries have signed the treaty. However, ten of these countries, including France, have not ratified it.

6 Renaud de Donnedieu Vabres's speech can be found at http://mistral.culture.fr/culture/actualites/conferen/donnedieu/estivada2006.html.

7 The other five venues were *Cabaret d'Oc, Castanbada, Contaire, Imatge*, as well as (in French) *Théâtre*. This information appeared on the program and on the map of the festival.

8 http://www.estivada-rodez.com/acceil.php, in the section "L'Occitanie, une civilisation à re-connaître."

9 http://www.estivada-rodez.com/acceil.php, in the section "La civilisation occitane, un projet de société."

10 Eco mentions countries; in the present context, one might refer to regions.

11 There exists a vast literature on the Félibrige. Frédéric Mistral's *Discours de Mistral* is rich in details about the militant agenda of the movement.

WORKS CITED

Bauman, Zygmunt. *Community: Seeking Safety in an Insecure World*. Cambridge: Polity Press, 2003.

Calin, William. *Minority Literatures and Modernism: Scots, Breton, and Occitan, 1920-1990*. Toronto: University of Toronto Press, 2000.

Council of Europe, Local and Regional Democracy, Legal Affairs. http://conventions. coe.int/treaty/Commun/ChercheSig.asp?NT=148&CM=1&DF=&CL=ENG. Accessed 4 September 2007.

Donnedieu Vabres, Renaud de. "Lancement du Festival Estivada à Rodez, 18 juillet 2006" http://mistral.culture.fr/culture/actualites/conferen/donnedieu/estivada2006.html. Accessed 4 September 2007.

Eco, Umberto. "Dreaming of the Middle Ages." *Travels in Hyperreality* Trans. William Weaver. San Diego: Harcourt, Brace, Jovanovich, 1986. 61-72.

_____. "A Theory of Expositions." *Travels in Hyperreality*. Trans. William Weaver. San Diego: Harcourt, Brace, Jovanovich, 1986. 73-85.

European Charter for Regional_and Minority Languages. http://www.coe.int/T/E/Legal_Affaires/Local_and_regional_Democracy/Regional_or_Minority_Languages Accessed 5 February 2008.

Estivada. http://www.estivada-rodez.com/acceil.php Accessed 4 September 2007.

Gardy, Philippe. "Okzitanien, eine Arena." *Entfremdung, Sebstsbefreiung und Norm. Texte aus der okzitanischen Soziolinguistik*. Ed. Georg Kremnitz. Tübingen: Narr, 1982. 152-67.

_____. *L'écriture occitane contemporaine: une quête des mots*. Paris: Editions de l'Harmattan, 1996.

JanMohamed, Abdul and David Lloyd. "Introduction: Toward a Theory of Minority Discourse. What Is To Be Done?" *The Nature and Context of Minority Discourse*. Eds Abdul JanMohamed and David Lloyd. New York: Oxford UP, 1990. 1-16.

Kremnitz, Georg. "Langue littéraire et langue parlée en Occitan." *Langues, dialects et écriture: Les langues romanes de France*. Eds Hervé Guillorel and Jean Sibille. Paris: IEO/IPIE, 1993. 240-46.

Lury, Celia. *Prosthetic Culture: Photography, Memory and Identity*. London: Routledge, 1998.

Mistral, Frédéric. *Discours de Mistral*. Aix-en-Provence: Félibrige, 1941.

Picard, David and Mike Robinson. "Remaking Worlds: Festivals, Tourism and Change." *Festivals, Tourism and Social Change: Remaking Worlds*. Eds David Picard and Mike Robinson. Clevedon: Channel View Publications, 2006. 1-31.

Renan, Ernest. "What Is a Nation? (1882)" *Nations and Identities: Classic Readings*. Ed. Vincent P. Pecora. Trans. William G. Hutchinson. Oxford: Blackwell, 2001. 162-76.

Sontag, Susan. *On Photography*. New York: Anchor, 1977.

The Cult of Mary Magdalene:
Symbol-Allegory in Medieval and Modern Devotional Literature

Matthew D. O'Donnell

Umberto Eco outlines the theoretical foundations of neomedievalism in "The Return of the Middle Ages," contrasting "dreaming" the Middle Ages with "living" the effects of the Middle Ages in the present-day world. Eco describes neomedievalism as "an age of 'permanent transition'...a culture of constant readjustment, fed on utopia...not so much...that of preserving the past scientifically as of developing hypotheses for the exploitation of disorder, entering into the logic of conflictuality" (84). He draws a parallel between medieval and neomedieval scholarly preservation, calling both "a constant retranslation and reuse" of the available literary heritage without any systematic preservation, neither archiving the past nor discarding it; instead, he explains how modern scholars evoke a strikingly medieval form of literary analysis, making "a heedless destruction and a disordered preservation...an immense work of bricolage, balanced among nostalgia, hope, and despair" (84). In modern popular literature concerning Mary Magdalene's role in the Bible and her place in Christianity, numerous interpretations of the saint re-envision her as the thirteenth apostle (often conflated with the *apostola apostolorum* of medieval Catholic tradition), the "Tower of the Faith" (deciphering *Magdalene* as the Hebrew *Migdal-eder*), or as a representative of the elusive divine feminine (due to the *hieros gamos* tradition of ancient Egypt and Mesopotamia). While there is no direct medieval counterpart to this modern devotion to the Magdalene, what sustains this *bricolage* of ancient explanations of a modern desire for feminine divinity is nonetheless an intuitive use of symbol-allegory similar in function to the allegorical biblical interpretations that sustained the popular Cathar heresy in southern France during the flourish of Languedoc culture in the late twelfth and early thirteenth centuries. It is this revitalization of a medieval practice, then, that increases the impact of the Magdalene in modern society, and shows the continuing importance of medieval ways of thinking in modern academic and popular culture.

The functions of medieval allegory are illuminated in the theories of several modern scholars, notably those of R.W. Frank Jr. and Bainard Cowan. Frank's study of the different types of medieval allegory includes both personification-allegory, which focuses on personified representations of abstract concepts (such as the Rose in the *Roman de la Rose*), and symbol-allegory, wherein concrete literary figures or characters are given an "other value" that is not inherent in the figure or persona itself: "the other value for the symbols and their pattern of relationship (and activity) must be worked out from either the narrower context of the work itself or the wider context of relevant biographical and historical facts and contemporary ideas and ideologies" (Frank 241). Cowan's incisive examination of Benjaminian literary allegory further underscores the separation between the interpretation of a text and the text itself: "The affirmation of the *existence* of truth, then, is the first precondition for allegory; the second is the recognition of its *absence*. Allegory could not exist if truth were accessible: as a mode of expression it arises in perpetual response to the human condition of being exiled from the truth that it would embrace" (114, original emphasis). The interpretation of symbol-allegory, whether medieval or modern, seems to hinge upon the very lack of an objective explanation of a particular passage containing obscure images or diverse interpretations; or, as Frank explains, the interpretation of a particular passage can be in and of itself a voyage of discovery for the potential initiate into more esoteric brands of knowledge:

> The writer, of course, does not always explain. Sometimes he may feel it is artistically clumsy to explain. Sometimes it might be dangerous (true of political symbol-allegory in particular). Sometimes he can rely (or thinks he can) on his audience to understand his other meaning. Sometimes he may wish to be understood by a select few and no one else. Or finally, sometimes he is a mystic and cannot describe his experience literally, [so] symbols are his only language (241).

This same separation between the "truth" of a concrete literary image and any allegorical interpretations by later scholars persists in the transition from medieval to modern culture, where the essential "message," as Eco would have it, behind many heresies, mystery cults, and esoteric traditions has been lost due to systematic persecution and the enforcement of dogmatic interpretations by a cultural and literary hierarchy (Eco 71). Yet, rather than being handicaps of a scholarly nature, these fundamental absences of essential "truths" necessitate allegorical detective-work to fill in the gaps left in the text, reduced by time to an untranslatable residue. Synthesizing diverse and often esoteric religious material was a specialty of medieval scholars, as demonstrated by the syncretism of the early Catholic Church in encouraging pagan converts, and by the intellectual zeal of medieval mystery cults and allegory-dependent heresies such as the Languedoc Cathars in making doctrinal sense of obscure myths and stories. The use of medieval allegorical traditions provides a fertile landscape for understanding the growing popularity of alternative theologies and esoteric culture, as in modern popular devotional texts like *The Da Vinci Code* and *The Goddess in the Gospels*, which already have a great deal of popular support and, one might say, a nearly heretical religious following.

Parallels to these popular traditions in modern-day Europe and America can be found in the religious and cultural flowering of the medieval Languedoc region of modern-day France. It is well established that the various religious schools subsumed into the Catholic faith prior to the fall of the Roman Empire "proposed or repudiated ideas that worked their way into Christianity, either openly or covertly, irrespective of their orthodoxy or even heterodoxy" (Fichtenau 105).[1] Notable among the imports into southern France is the Bogomil-inspired dualism, anticlerical reform and apostolic asceticism of the *Cathari*, the "pure ones." Having begun as a small intellectual movement in Italy, the Cathar message of purification energized the people of Languedoc against the indolent and hypocritical clergy, paving the way for the artistic and cultural independence that has often been called a mini-Renaissance in the twelfth and thirteenth centuries. Especially interesting is the fact that "the Cathars assimilated the most diverse biblical parables into their central myth," not out of a "mania for innovation," but because Cathar preachers essentially lacked the foundational "truth" of a unique religious text (Fichtenau 168). Instead, Cathar dualism had to be grafted onto Christian monotheism, using whatever sources or interpretations were necessary to satisfy the "central myth" of warring kingdoms of heaven and hell fighting over earth as an inherently justified theological belief system. Allegorization of previous religious literature (in this case, the Bible) was not just important to the Cathar heresy—it was essential to the survival of the Cathar faith to have a literary source in which to ground the group's morality.[2]

It is also possible to view modern allegorical interpretations of the Magdalene as reviving this same necessity for allegorical interpretation. From Margaret Starbird's work on recapturing the feminine principle of divinity in medieval worship to Dan Brown's infectious novelization of Magdalene worship and its supposed connections to the mythology of the Holy Grail, the rigid authority of scholarly investigation has as yet been unable to stem the tide of allegorization of the Magdalene as a modern figure of veneration and a symbol of feminine oppression within the male-dominated Church. In our era of scientific investigation and computational reasoning, it is not difficult to recognize an analogous sort of orthodoxy among scholarly "clergy" concerning popular movements such as veneration of Mary Magdalene in popular literature, where supposedly unrelated events in biblical literature become symbolic of a seemingly under-represented feminine role in Christian worship. Yet, in Claire Nahmad and Margaret Bailey's *The Secret Teachings of Mary Magdalene*, the difference is tangible between what are scholarly (and thus historically-based) analyses and the intuitive, pious, and surprisingly religious methods of inner discovery that Nahmad and Bailey use to uncover the "secrets" of Magdalene veneration: "We always look for confirmation that we have got the message right as far as we can, and search deep within ourselves via meditation, prayer, and clarification from the outer world in the form of the more usual methods of research that what we are hearing with our inner ears really does apply" (xii). It is worth noting that Dante himself intimated to his patron Can Grande della Scala the importance of allegory as a necessary counterpart to purely historical interpretation: "And although these mystical meanings are called by various names, they may one and all in a general sense be termed allegorical, in as much as they are different from the literal or historical" (XIII.22). This modern tension between using textual evidence to the exclusion of spiritual intuition and the inclusion of allegorical methods of inquiry to elucidate further meanings of the text at hand mirrors the development of literary analysis in the late Middle Ages, when close reading first came to prominence.

Whereas "virtually all the theological scholarship produced before the twelfth century" grew out of the patristic affection for allegorical interpretation of the Bible and the various mystery cults with widely varying doctrines based on similar biblical passages, in the later Middle Ages literal interpretation had begun to supplant allegorical interpretation (Fichtenau 206).[3] Curiously, Cathar allegorical argumentation may have played a deciding role in the focus on interpretation *ad litteram* among the scholars of the time: "In dealing with the heretics, one had to stick strictly to the Gospel texts. As Joachim of Fiore asserted, 'They falsify [the text] by misunderstanding the meaning of the words'" (Fichtenau 210, original insertion). When modern scholars discuss figures such as Mary Magdalene, the conversation is weighted in favor of historiographical analysis and remnants of textual evidence, while the widely circulated literary and popular transformations of the Magdalene's story are given less credence:

> Here is not merely a conflated Mary—the individual parts are taken from discrete Gospel accounts, most of which are not actually about her—but also an imagined Mary...Even if we are also interested in knowing what the actual, historical Mary was like, based on the flimsy evidence that survives about her, it is important to realize that she came to be remembered in this way...With Mary we are dealing not only with how an important woman was remembered in the years and centuries after her death but also with how she was remembered by *men* (Ehrman 191).

Simultaneously citing the "historical" and deriding the "flimsy" literature concerning the character Mary Magdalene, Bart Ehrman seeks to discover the historical veracity of Mariam of Magdala while also divorcing Mary Magdalene from the millennia of interpretation and veneration that this character inspired, including the continuing inspiration taken from her stories today. Instead of the wide and varied corpus of Magdalene literature and devotional study, there remains an enforcement of academic (clerkly) hierarchy on an inherently popular religious tradition, a codification of academic faith that tends to alienate some of the more colourful connections modern devotees make when allegorizing the symbol of the Magdalene in the service of their individual beliefs.[4]

The social struggles embedded in twelfth-century politics between France and Languedoc add to the discussion of possible causes for the rise of Catharism in southern France and provide insight into our modern academic heritage: "Considering the wealth of this part of Europe and the vitality of its culture, its increasing defection from the Catholic Church threatened a schism in the Christian world of the greatest significance....[T]he Albigensian domination of southern France constituted a cancer in the body of European civilization which had to be rooted out at all costs" (Cantor 417). This grassroots political shift away from centralized papal power is emphasized in "The Song of the Cathar Wars," a thirteenth century Provençal historical epic begun by William of Tudela, a supporter of the dogmatic northern crusaders led by Simon de Montfort, and completed by an anonymous supporter of the people of Languedoc and their defender, Raymond of Toulouse. During a pivotal battle in the second (Albigensian) half of the poem, Raymond has returned to defend his stolen castle at Toulouse from the absent Montfort. Notably, he enlists the entirety of Toulouse to work side-by-side to build defences against the crusaders:

> Never in any town have I seen such magnificent labourers, for the counts were hard at work there, with all the knights, the citizens and their wives and valiant merchants, men, women and courteous money-changers, small children, boys and girls, servants, running messengers, every one of them joined eagerly in the work (Shirley 124).

By championing the cause of the Toulousain people and equitably working alongside the peasantry, the nobility have ensured their people's safety; the crusaders are thus hierarchically unprepared for the resistance of the city they believed to be a gift directly from the pope: "'Well, my lords,' said Sir Alan in retreat, 'I see you are thoroughly beaten! Knights, who can have defeated us? France is disgraced, our glory lost, we are conquered by a beaten country! Better unborn, better not to have lived, than to be defeated like this by unarmed men!'" (126). It seems from this popular rendition that political independence, even more than religious doctrine, might have helped give rise to the Cathar strain of dualism in southern France; according to Fichtenau, "the text alone reflects...the violent conflict against the heretics in southern France. Indeed, in many respects, that dispute qualified as a civil war" (168).

From the position of the Albigensian crusaders, the goal of heresy suppression was actually the enforcement of orthodoxy and the elimination of heterodoxy. Stoyanov relates how Cathar dualism became vilified through inquisitorial investigation: "With the gradual demonization of the medieval dualists and the orthodox assimilation of heresy to witchcraft, Cathar dualism was to play a very important role in the very shaping of the medieval concept of witchcraft" (189). The differing doctrines of the Languedoc Cathars and the Balkan Bogomils only exacerbated their lack of connection to the relative safety of Church dogma, as medieval dualists had multiple interpretations of warring light and dark kingdoms laid like a *bricolage* over the top of the established Christian mythology:

> The Cathars assimilated the most diverse biblical parables into their central myth....Due in part to the illiteracy of many believers, a passage might come to be imbued with an almost indelible nature, as if it were an aphorism and not a statement that could be properly understood only in the narrative and didactic context of a Gospel or Epistle (Fichtenau 168).

In modern times the allegorical method by which Cathars substantiated their mythology has become scholastically quaint, a supposed "mania for innovation," where "no real attempt [is] made to bridge the gap between myth and reason," but Frank observes that medieval Cathars were certainly in the majority of biblical exegetes for using allegories to understand Christian literature: "The medieval Church constantly stimulated [the] imagination with both symbols and abstractions. In giving allegorical interpretations to the Scriptures and to beasts, flowers, jewels, etc., the Church created a mode of thought which encouraged symbol-allegory" (239).[5] Fundamentally, Cathar dualism pursued the same aims as orthodox Christianity; what Cathars lacked, it seems, was neither ingenuity nor rationality but merely the textual foundations to support their mythical claims, the written evidence for their views on creation.[6]

In much the same manner, pursuers of the Magdalene in modern times have no dearth of faith in their search, but often a distinct lack of satisfactory texts for a religiously satisfying heterodoxy of Christianity; thus, modern devotees are often required to pursue any and all interpretations, including allegorical and mystical ones, to codify their beliefs in Christian terms. Margaret Starbird, in her *Goddess in the Gospels*, recounts her nervous breakdown and brief stay in a psychiatric ward, attributing symbolic meaning to incongruous elements during her stay:

> I did a double-take. *Why was there a crutch in a psychiatrist's office, resting against the stem of a large potted palm plant?* I wondered. In my mind, the crutch was an allusion to the wounded and crippled Bridegroom/King Jesus, bereft of his Bride, and the palm tree seemed symbolic of Israel and the royal house of David. I remembered that people spread palm branches before Jesus on his entry into Jerusalem, and called him Son of David. The palm tree is *phoenix* in Greek, like the mythical bird resurrected from the ashes. This bird, too, is a symbol for Christ (95).

Starbird's images are illuminated by a series of swift and well-placed symbol-allegories: that of the wounded Bridegroom (a mixed metaphor including both Chrétien de Troyes' wounded Fisher-King and the Bridegroom of the Song of Songs, both of whom share allegorical connections with Cathar-influenced troubadours and popular veneration of the Song of Songs in the churches of the Languedoc) and the palm tree/phoenix (its etymological and mythic associations with both the Davidic line of Jewish kings and Christ's resurrection being well documented by Starbird and others). Her conversion narrative is similarly heresiarchic: in several passages, she decries the masculine myopia of the "Logos-oriented" Catholic Church:

> The formidable institution called "the Church" was based on former patriarchal religions and their worship of a sun-god principle...it was shepherded by a privileged priesthood reluctant to share power...They and the altars they served are declared holy, set apart. They came to resemble the privileged god-kings of the pagan temples, like those of Egypt and Babylon (107).

Here, the focus is not simply on a Protestant-style reformation of the Church, but a revelation of the inherently flawed and idolatrous nature of the present Catholic Church, "an idol that turns the garden of God into a shriveled wasteland" (107-08). One could hardly ask for a more Cathar distinction between the devil-controlled earthly church and the heavenly Kingdom outside of the realm of earthly matters. Starbird contrasts what she believes to be a misogynist version of Christianity by focusing on the traditions surrounding Mary Magdalene and the cathartic potential of a modern Magdalene heresy: "The new revelation we received destroyed the authoritarian, strong-man father image, turning it to ashes...my closest friends and I had not lost our faith. We were only being purified and healed of toxic illusions...the time had come to purify our understanding of 'the Holy One,' to cleanse the altars of our hearts so long defiled by idolatrous 'sun' worship" (108).[7]

Today the "orthodox" view of high scholastic enquiry encompasses the more scientific method of literary analysis that became popular in the late medieval period and became emblematic of Renaissance thought: interpretation *ad litteram*, which values loyalty to the sole authority of the text over the popular faith of the congregation. What remains more important for our modern devotees is the *un*orthodox view, the specifically *heterodox* view of a faith-centered exploration of biblical and medieval traditions in response to the largely hierarchical and dogmatic environment of academic research, caricatured as staid and sterile in comparison to the vital popular support for the Magdalene in the modern devotional community. As the expanding corpus of popular veneration shows, modern devotees appear to have reasserted some measure of control over their sacred literature, reinterpreting ancient biblical accounts using the same allegorical tools as the medieval Cathars to create a full-fledged modern heresy centered around Mary Magdalene and her role in the fundamental structure of Christian mythos. Time will tell how the established scholarly community receives these new heretics and their distinctly neomedieval take on a centuries-old process of spiritual inquiry.

UNIVERSITY OF GEORGIA

NOTES

1 See Elaine Pagels, whose *Beyond Belief* and *The Gnostic Gospels* examines at length the political and social upheavals of early Christianity and their focus on shaping Christianity (and its "heretical" detractors) into a world-class religion.

2 See Raphael Patai's *The Hebrew Goddess* for a detailed account of the Kabbalistic allegorization of the Torah in an effort to provide similar textual grounding for an alternative scholarly understanding of Judaism.

3 Fichtenau notes, "Jerome spoke for all biblical exegetes when he stated: 'Each and every sentence, syllable, letter, and comma in God's writings is replete with meaning.' Origen, who championed the allegorical method, believed that it was extraordinarily difficult, if not impossible, to ascertain these meanings down to the last detail; Augustine referred to the Bible as the 'book of mysteries.' Their search for meaning resembled that of the Gnostics and the Platonists" (206).

4 Some chapter and appendix titles of Nahmad and Bailey's book include "The Virgin Birth and Isis on Earth," "The Triple Goddess," "The Dragon Queen," and "Mary's Secret Sign and the Mystery of the Chakras."

5 Dante describes the Four Levels of reading in his *Epistole XIII* to Cangrande della Scala: *Et primus dicitur litteralis, secundus vero allegoricus, sive moralis, sive anagogicus* (XIII.20).

6 According to Fichtenau, "Later on, important elements of [Cathar] doctrine became overgrown with allegorization...Christ's miracles were given allegorical interpretations,

as were biblical passages concerning marriage, which were said to refer to either Christ and the church, or the bishop and his flock, or the body and the soul. How one chose to interpret marriage was not as important as one's renunciation of the institution in principle. No one even objected to contradictory interpretations as long as they served the proper ends" (170-71).

7 Starbird initially struggles with her apostasy, saying "I did not want to be a heretic, out on a limb by myself—scorned and shunned" (112).

WORKS CITED

Alighieri, Dante. "*Epistole XIII* to Cangrande della Scala." The Princeton Dante Project, ed. Ermenegildo Pistelli, trans. Paget Toynbee. Princeton University. 2 June 2008. <http://etcweb.princeton.edu/dante/pdp/>

Cantor, Norman F. *Medieval History: The Life and Death of a Civilization.* 2nd ed. London: Macmillan, 1969.

Cowan, Bainard. "Walter Benjamin's Theory of Allegory," *New German Critique* 22 (1981): 109-22.

Eco, Umberto. *Travels in Hyperreality: Essays.* Trans. William Weaver. San Diego: Harcourt Brace Jovanovich, 1986.

Ehrman, Bart D. *Peter, Paul, and Mary Magdalene.* Oxford: Oxford UP, 2006.

Fichtenau, Heinrich. *Heretics and Scholars in the High Middle Ages 1000-1200.* Trans. Denise A. Kaiser. University Park, PA: Pennsylvania State UP, 1998.

Frank, R[obert] W[orth], Jr. "The Art of Reading Medieval Personification-Allegory." *ELH* 20.4 (1953): 237-50.

Nahmad, Claire, and Margaret Bailey. *The Secret Teachings of Mary Magdalene.* London: Watkins, 2006.

Pagels, Elaine. *Beyond Belief: The Secret Gospel of Thomas.* New York: Random House, 2003.

_____. *The Gnostic Gospels.* New York: Vintage, 1979.

Shirley, Janet, trans. *The Song of the Cathar Wars.* Brookfield: Ashgate, 1996.

Starbird, Margaret. *The Goddess in the Gospels.* Rochester: Bear & Co., 1998.

Stoyanov, Yuri. *The Hidden Tradition in Europe.* London: Penguin Arkana, 1994.

Truth, Fiction, and Freedom: The Harrowing of Hell in Philip Pullman's *The Amber Spyglass* and Ursula Le Guin's *The Other Wind*

Ruth Wehlau

The story of the Harrowing of Hell, Christ's descent into the underworld to conquer Satan and death and to free the dead from their bondage, was an important part of Christian mythology in the Middle Ages, where it appeared in the mystery plays and multiple other vernacular representations. Recently, versions of the Harrowing have re-emerged in two contemporary fantasy novels published within a year of each other—Philip Pullman's *The Amber Spyglass* (2000) and Ursula Le Guin's *The Other Wind* (2001).[1] Both novels re-work the story, freely adapting themes and elements of the narrative, while divorcing the myth from its Christian setting. Both authors use the myth in a way that reflects the power of the original story, representing freedom from fear of death as a response to the problem of evil.

The doctrine of the Harrowing of Hell evolved in conjunction with other early Christian notions of Hell.[2] The Harrowing clearly incorporates the descent topos found throughout myth, romance, and epic (such as *Beowulf* or *The Aeneid*), but it involves much more than this: it also includes the conquest of death itself and the release of the dead, all carried out by a messianic figure. This differentiates it from the Orpheus myth, where the descent is occasioned by the desire to save one particular individual from death. The Harrowing represents communal rather than individual salvation, and is essentially a way of addressing the problem of human mortality: Adam and Eve's fall brings death into the world; Christ's destruction of death and rescue of the dead restores and renews the world, overturning the effects of the Fall.[3] Overall, the Harrowing brings about a rebirth or renewal—a fundamental change in the fabric of the cosmos and the human condition.

The essential elements of the Harrowing can be described as a) a messiah, b) a descent into the underworld, c) the conquest of death, and d) the release of the dead.[4] Both Pullman's and Le Guin's novels include Harrowings that contain most of these elements—a messianic character in each, a descent of sorts, followed by a release of the dead. Those characters that are messianic conform to the Christian pattern: their advents have been prophesied, and their roles as liberators of the dead are constructed partly through suffering or sacrifice. Both liberators are also associated with fire, the highest of the elements and the one most frequently connected to transformation and divine power. However, in several ways, the Harrowings in the two novels differ significantly from medieval Harrowings. In each, the release of the dead is effected by a partnership of two people, a male and a female (surrounded by a larger supporting group), and in each novel the central messianic character is a female: an adolescent girl in *The Amber Spyglass*, and a young woman in *The Other Wind*. Furthermore, both novels draw indirectly on the myth of Orpheus as the original impulse behind the Harrowing.

The Amber Spyglass is the concluding book in Philip Pullman's trilogy, *His Dark Materials*—novels that encompass a Blakean revision of Milton's *Paradise Lost*, "reversing the moral polarities" of Milton, as Pullman describes it (Colbert 10).[5] *His Dark Materials* can also be seen as a narrative response to C.S. Lewis, since Pullman has been outspoken in objecting to the Narnia stories, which he claims are misogynistic and racist and which, according to Pullman, deny the value of the passage to adulthood (Miller 72). In contrast, *His Dark Materials* celebrates the adolescent coming into adulthood, and rejects the puritanical—or even Manichean—aspects of the traditional Christian attitude toward sex that Pullman feels are inherent in Lewis' novels. Pullman explicitly turns Christian mythology upside down, depicting his heroine, an adolescent girl named Lyra "Silvertongue" Belacqua, as the new Eve. In Pullman's trilogy, sexuality, the female, and adolescence are positive, not sinful; equally important for him is the art of storytelling itself, which plays a key role in the Harrowing scene and elsewhere.[6]

It is Lyra who frees the dead in *The Amber Spyglass*. Her father, Lord Asriel, is the leader of the revolt in heaven and thus, from a Christian point of view, Lyra is a daughter to the father of lies. Lyra herself is a proficient fabulator, a teller of stories, a liar (as implied by her name), and this is an important aspect of her role as liberator of the dead. When Lyra reaches the entrance of the underworld, her way is blocked by harpies who torment the dead with terrible tales that provoke grief and remorse in their minds. Lyra, who has delighted her dead travelling companions with wonderful made-up stories, attempts to tell the same kind of fiction to the harpies and is immediately attacked. Eventually, Lyra tells the true story of her adventures; this enthralls the harpies, and she is allowed to pass. Pullman has explained this passage as an illustration of the fact that fantasy alone is not enough, that fiction must have a core of truth.[7] Lyra herself is associated with truth as well as with lies; she alone can read the alethiometer (the "truth meter") instinctively and without difficulty, and she initially seeks out the land of the dead for the sake of one particular person, in this case a friend that she has inadvertently betrayed into the hands of death, so that her behavior is a kind of exemplum of truth.

Truth and lying are linked in other ways in Pullman's underworld. If Lyra's name alludes to her skill as a liar, it also evokes the lyre, and thus the transformative power of art that allowed Orpheus to enter Hades. Lyra's stories are powerful indeed: her artful account of her journey assuages the harpies and allows her to enter the land of the dead. However, stories are also an aspect of Hell's falsity: the harpies, by haranguing the dead with tales about the crimes and sins they committed during their lives, tell only one side of the story and thus only a half-truth. After Lyra's reconciliation with the harpies, she asks them to tell the dead stories about good things, to evoke positive memories, and also to listen to the stories of the dead themselves—those who speak truth will be released from Hell. Stories are then one means by which the dead are released, not only from the underworld, but also from grief and remorse. The

Harrowing that results is a transformation based on the very notion of story, and effected by Lyra who, like fiction itself, is both a liar and a truth-teller.

The land of the dead portrayed in Pullman's novel is based largely on the underworld of classical epic. The dead are shadows without substance, their domain a wasteland where nothing happens. Over time the dead forget their own names, but they are able to talk and reason. The pathos of the situation is increased by the fact that the dead people portrayed in Pullman's work are primarily children, apparently alone and abandoned. Despite its misery, Pullman's underworld is what Alan Bernstein calls "neutral," where the dead are not sorted in any way.[8] Neither the abyss nor the land of the dead *per se* is controlled by any particular God or overseer and the only laws are those of physics—most obviously the force of gravity. On their way out of the land of the dead, the ghosts, led by Lyra, must pass close to the edge of the abyss. At one point, Lyra stumbles and nearly falls down into the abyss herself; she survives only because she is rescued by the harpy No Name.

The alternative to this combination of underworld wasteland and abyss is described when Lyra offers to free the dead. This represents a return to life, the life of the cosmos, but in a new form—a purely physical absorption into cosmic matter. Lyra explains what this will involve in a speech replete with the rhetoric of truth and honour:

> "This is what'll happen," she said, "and it's true, perfectly true. When you go out of here, all the particles that make you up will loosen and float apart, just like your daemons did. If you've seen people dying, you know what that looks like. But your daemons en't just nothing now; they're part of everything. All the atoms that were them, they've gone into the air and the wind and the trees and the earth and all the living things. They'll never vanish. They're just part of everything. And that's exactly what'll happen to you, I swear to you, I promise on my honor" (319).

Lyra's urgent assertion signals a new reality, a cosmos that consists of a new opposition, not heaven opposed to hell, with earth in between; instead, the meaningless existence in the underworld/abyss is contrasted to the very matter of creation, of life. In like manner, Pullman concludes his novel with a reference to the Republic of Heaven, a democracy to be built on earth rather than a kingdom to be sought after death. The ultimate contrast, however, lies not in opposing worlds, but in the stories that are told about these worlds. The old Christian truths of heaven and hell are proven to be lies, while the new truth is found in Lyra's forceful argument for a purely materialist understanding of the afterlife. Pullman's own tale, the novel, is presented as a new story, a new truth that releases everyone from the ancient lies, the punitive narratives of traditional Christianity.

Like Pullman's *The Amber Spyglass*, Ursula Le Guin's *The Other Wind* concludes a series—in this case, the Earthsea stories. Where Pullman's reversal of Christian mythology might be termed architectonic, Le Guin's approach is organic. Her Earthsea series originally formed a trilogy ending with a descent into the land of the dead in her novel, *The Farthest Shore*. After this, Le Guin added two more novels and a book of short stories set in Earthsea,[9] the last of which is *The Other Wind*, which revisits the land of the dead in an episode that is no longer just a descent, but a Harrowing. Unlike Pullman, Le Guin does not reverse the Christian narrative so much as she deconstructs it, borrowing its imagery and rebuilding it in an entirely new form. Fire is not an element of Hell in Le Guin's novel; rather, it is a positive transformative force. Likewise, the dragon, found in various forms throughout Christianity and always demonized (most notably as the mouth of Hell itself), is primarily positive for Le Guin, especially in her later work.

There are two people directly involved in releasing the dead in *The Other Wind*. The first is a man, Alder, who is haunted by the dead and connected to them through his bond with his dead wife. In this respect, he is an Orpheus-like character, and as in *The Amber Spyglass*, it is the bond between two individuals that instigates the Harrowing. The second is a woman, Tehanu. In the previous novel of the series, we learn that Tehanu was thrown into a fire and left to die before being rescued and adopted: in other words, she has suffered a symbolic crucifixion and rebirth (Le Guin, *Tehanu* 1-6).[10] Significantly, her hand is burnt and permanently damaged so that like Christ, Tehanu bears the marks of her suffering on her body. She also embodies a miraculous duality similar to the hypostatic union, which is the perfect union of human and divine in Christ according to Christian theology. Tehanu's father is a dragon, although she herself appears to be the product of a human birth; however, she seems to be more dragon than human, a departure from the Christian parallel. Like Lyra, Tehanu is marked by her "tongue"—although in this case, by her silence, not by her storytelling ability. She speaks only rarely for years after her initial rescue from the fire, perhaps because of the trauma, but also because human speech, inherently symbolic, is not her true language. Rather, her native tongue is the Old Speech, the language of the dragons.

In the Earthsea novels, dragons are portrayed as powerful, threatening, and alien beings who are immortal and capable of moving between worlds. Their most significant feature may be their language, which Le Guin portrays as containing a reality excluded from human language. Where human languages are symbolic and differentiated from each other, there is only one dragon language, the Old Speech, also called "the Language of the Making," which contains the true names of all things. The Old Speech is essential and performative, a point of access to ultimate reality. The fiery nature of the dragons, destructive but also creative, is part of this underlying and transcendent reality, and the dragons themselves represent both truth and freedom for Le Guin, as she makes clear in an earlier discussion of fantasy fiction: "fantasy is true, of course. It isn't factual, but it's true....[Adults] are afraid of dragons, because they are afraid of freedom" ("Dragons" 44).[11]

When the novel begins, the world of Earthsea is undergoing a change. Dragons are invading the lands of the humans and magic is beginning to disappear. Eventually, it is determined that at one time, one group of humans—

the Hardic people of the Archipelago—made use of magic in order to avoid death by remaining forever as ghostly beings in the land of the dead, a land which was introduced in the first Earthsea novel as a place behind a low wall. Subsequently, in the third Earthsea novel, *The Farthest Shore*, the heroes Ged and Lebannen travel to the land of the dead.[12] As in the short story, "The Word of Unbinding," this land is depicted as a static place outside of the normal motions of the cosmos, a place of eternal night where the stars do not move. Here it is separated from the land of the living not only by the wall, but also by "the Mountains of Pain" (*Shore* 171-87). The land is a barren wasteland, referred to as the Dry Land, where the dead wander in a permanent state of mindlessness, unable to recognize or respond to the living or to each other, an existence so horrible that it seems to contradict the dominant message of all of Le Guin's work: that death is a part of the world, and should be accepted as such. It appears that Le Guin herself came to this realization sometime after writing the first three books of the series, and that *The Other Wind*, written many years later, is an attempt to rectify the problem. In *The Other Wind*, we discover that the Dry Land has been stolen from the dragons. It is an artificial construction, created by humans, and the wall of death that divides this land from the living is "a false wall" (197).

As a purely human construct, the false wall is the opposite of the reality represented by the dragons. Moreover, since the walled-off Dry Land is stolen, it is a symbol of treachery and the human tendency to overreach. At the novel's end, Irian, another dragon in human form, speaks scornfully to the human magicians:

> You own the earth, you own the sea. But we are the fire of sunlight, we fly the wind! You wanted land to own. You wanted things to make and keep. And you have that. That was the division, the *verw nadan*. But you were not content with your share. You wanted not only your cares, but our freedom. You wanted the wind! And by the spells and wizardries of those oath-breakers, you stole half our realm from us, walled it away from life and light, so that you could live there forever. Thieves, traitors! (194)

For Le Guin, the wall is false because it is impossible to maintain—it is contrary to the laws of the cosmos—but also because it is delusory, a literal representation of false consciousness. The very attempt to control the physical world through symbolic exchange—magic, art, language—is at fault. The sterile dark land is the result of the human desire to claim what does not belong to humanity.

Le Guin is less precise than Pullman on the specifics of where the dead go once released. Perhaps they have entered the world of the purely material, but there is another possibility. One group, the Kargish people, have kept alive the true story about the Hardic magicians' theft of dragon land. They themselves have chosen to reject this artificial death; instead they believe in reincarnation, a belief also suggested in the words of Tehanu as she and Alder begin the destruction of the wall:

I think that when I die, I can breathe back the death that made me
live. I can give back to the world all that I didn't do. All that I might
have been and couldn't be. All the choices I didn't make. All the things
I lost and spent and wasted. I can give them back to the world. To
the lives that haven't been lived yet. That will be my gift back to the
world that gave me the life I did live, the love I loved, the breath I
breathed (197-8).

This kind of reincarnation is slightly different from Pullman's notion of death
as absorption into the cosmos, and yet similar in its focus on dissolution and
rebirth. In fact, Le Guin's novel hints at a kind of cosmic restoration, and it is
interesting to compare her treatment of this concept with an early Christian
formulation of death—Origen's notion of restoration or *apokatastasis*. Although
the notion of the afterlife that came to dominate Christianity is a moral one,
defined by Augustine's doctrine of two deaths—bodily death followed by a
second death at the time of judgment—it was not the only theory of the afterlife
(Bernstein 316-7). Strongly influenced by neoplatonism, Origen held that the
souls of the dead would be repeatedly cycled through the cosmos until they
eventually returned to God, and cosmic unity would prevail. Origen allowed
for the punishment of sins, but division into good and evil was less important
than the *apokatastasis* or restoration that was to come in the end (Bernstein
307). This aspect of death and the afterlife is strongly evoked in *The Other
Wind*, in which the two liberators—Alder and Tehanu—are both associated
with restoration. Alder is a magician, whose gift is that of fixing the broken,
and it is this deep power of his—the power of repair and reconstruction—that
makes him the conduit for the release of the dead. Tehanu is restored to
herself: at the novel's end, she goes off to live with the dragons, her body,
now a dragon's body, golden and whole. This symbolizes the clear separation
of dragon and human, while marking the separation of human and dragon as
a kind of cosmic re-creation.

Le Guin, like Pullman, treats the element of fiction or art as an important
aspect of the story. Le Guin herself has said that magic in the Earthsea novels
is a representation of art.[13] Thus Alder's "art" is what connects him to the dead,
what torments him, and what allows him to lead the others to the wall. But
art is also a part of the new world that humans must make for themselves. At
the end of the novel, Le Guin's characters discuss the effects of the change
occasioned by the destruction of the wall:

"I think maybe the division that was begun, and then betrayed, will
be completed at last," he said. "The dragons will go free, and leave
us here to the choice we made."
"The knowledge of good and evil," said Onyx. "The joy of making,
shaping," said Seppel. "Our mastery" (199).

One character is worried that "when the dragons go, our mastery will go with
them." Someone else replies, "No, I think not. They are the Making, yes. But
we learned the Making. We made it ours" (199). Although dragons initially
appear to be fundamentally alien, *The Other Wind* reveals them to be distantly

related to humans. The two races divided long ago, each race having chosen its own course—the dragons, essential freedom and power; the humans, the world of culture and symbolism. This division is based on a choice made in the distant past, but it is a genuine choice, not a fall. Thus, unlike the Hardic attempt to prevent death by constructing the false land of the dead, there is no need for punishment here, only a sense that humans must grow up and learn to construct their own world based on the art and culture they have chosen. They still need the creative fire of the dragons, but fortunately it is available to them, for they too are a part of the created world. The release of the dead marks the beginning of a new bargain with the dragons, as humans return to their own realm where art will function as compensation for the loss of the old lie, the belief that mortality could be overcome.

A major difference between the Christian version of the Harrowing and the versions in Pullman and Le Guin is that neither of the contemporary authors portrays a conquest. There is no one to fight, no power of evil external to humanity. Rather, each novel reveals that what is truly terrible is the notion of Hell itself, not "moral" Hell, where the dead are punished, but the neutral underworld that is in fact a horrible form of immortality.[14] In contrast to this false and undesirable afterlife, the notion of pure non-existence becomes appealing. Both writers portray the new afterlife as something slightly more than simple non-existence, however, offering a notion of return or renewal to compensate for the loss of the old afterlife. A sense of transcendence is found in the universe itself, either in Pullman's notion of the afterlife as a return to pure matter, or in Le Guin's dragons. Furthermore, both Tehanu and Lyra are associated with stars: Lyra is the name of a constellation, and Tehanu is the name of a fictional star.

It is unclear to what extent Pullman and Le Guin were conscious of the Christian Harrowing as they wrote. Pullman has said that he does not know much about the Harrowing and that it did "not figure in [his] reading" (Colbert 132). As a "Church of England atheist" (according to Pullman himself in Miller 57), however, his work is grounded in the Christian theology of which the Harrowing forms a part. Le Guin is usually surprised at attempts by critics to find Christian themes in her work. It is interesting to note, however, that in discussing Christian myth in science fiction, she distinguishes between "living" and "dead" uses of Christian mythology:

> For an example of the use of science fiction of a living religious mythos one may turn to the work of Cordwainer Smith, whose Christian beliefs are evident, I think, all through his work, in such motifs as the savior, the martyr, rebirth....Whether or not one is a Christian, one may admire wholeheartedly the strength and passion given the works by the author's living belief. In general, however, I think the critics' search for Christian themes in science fiction is sterile and misleading. For the majority of science fiction writers, the themes of Christianity are dead signs, not living symbols, and those who use them do so all

too often in order to get an easy emotional charge without working for it. ("Myth" 76)[15]

Le Guin's use of the Harrowing in *The Other Wind* is certainly not dead, nor is it Christian. By drawing on similar elements and structures without being Christian itself, it is a living myth, parallel to the Christian story, but not representing it. In this, both Le Guin and Pullman can be clearly distinguished from C.S. Lewis, whose Harrowing in *The Lion, the Witch and the Wardrobe*, like the Narnia books in general, is ultimately a representation of the Christian myth.[16]

It is perhaps even more interesting if neither Pullman nor Le Guin was influenced directly by the Christian version of the Harrowing, and that these two contemporary novelists re-invented the story almost simultaneously. Both authors' versions of the Harrowing story accord with Christian mythology by locating it at the conclusions of their novels and of the larger narratives the novels participate in. Of course, there are other elements at work here, thematic echoes that result from the connection between the Christian Harrowing and the genre of romance. The Harrowing is, after all, a descent, and is represented this way literally by Pullman and figuratively by Le Guin; thus the Orpheus myth evoked by both Alder's quest (founded in love), and Lyra's quest (founded in loyalty), is converted into a romance that parallels the Christian salvation narrative. Likewise, each novel ultimately revolves around that hallmark of romance, the experience of "growing up," as the loss of the afterlife and acceptance of death lead to maturity for individual characters and for the human race as a whole. Finally, by placing this episode at the end of their series of novels, both writers have in some sense "elevated" their stories to epic status.

Whether truly intertextual or not, both Pullman and Le Guin use their archetypal narrative to make truth claims. Where the authority for the Christian salvation narrative depends upon the divine source believed to have inspired the evangelists and theologians, in *The Amber Spyglass* and *The Other Wind*, the "living" myth authorizes itself, allowing Pullman and Le Guin to give their fictions the authority of soteriological myth, thus offering a humanist version of the Harrowing that functions both intra-textually and meta-textually. Intra-textually, the humanism resides in the fact that both novels present humans remaking the cosmos on their own, without divine assistance, as well as in the significant role played by language, art, and storytelling in the stories. However, the humanism is also meta-textual. In each novel, the Harrowing revolves around the destruction or re-writing of a false narrative. Like Lyra among the harpies, Pullman's narrative transforms Hell, replacing the old Christian "lie" with a new truth. Likewise, Le Guin's revision of her earlier novels through the Harrowing in *The Other Wind* "frees" the dead by telling a new story in a new novel, placing Le Guin herself in a position not unlike Lyra. The conflict between good and evil, insofar as it is portrayed in the versions of the Harrowing described here, is in fact a conflict between what is true and what is false; truth literally sets the dead free and, through our new understanding, frees the reader as well. The release of the dead still represents a communal release, but for both writers, it is now a release from false beliefs, effected by human art, through the novel itself.

QUEEN'S UNIVERSITY

NOTES

I would like to thank Shelley King for many conversations in which she provided me with information about Philip Pullman and encouraged me as I formulated the ideas in this paper.

1 I take all quotations from the following editions: Philip Pullman, *The Amber Spyglass* (Alfred Knopf, 2000) and Ursula Le Guin, *The Other Wind* (Ace Books, 2001).

2 The most thorough discussion of the doctrine of the Harrowing of Hell is found in J.A. MacCulloch's classic study, *The Harrowing of Hell* (1930). The Harrowing ultimately descends from Ugartic myth, specifically the battle between Baal and Yamm. See Levenson 9-10.

3 Here is Origen's description of the event:
Christ emptied Himself and took the form of a servant, and suffered the domination of the tyrant, being made obedient unto death, by which death He destroyed him that had the power of death, the devil, that He might free those held by death. For having bound the strong man and triumphed in His Cross, He entered his house, the house of death, Hades, and spoiled his goods, i.e. He drew forth the souls which he held. (qtd. in MacCulloch 228)

4 This list is my own, not MacCulloch's. MacCulloch also includes a list of the elements of the Harrowing (198), but it is less helpful for this study.

5 Other useful critical work on Pullman's trilogy is found in Squires and in the collection of essays edited by Lenz and Scott.

6 For a discussion of the importance of storytelling to Pullman, and within his trilogy, see Squires 90-114.

7 Pullman states: "Lyra learns to her great cost that fantasy isn't enough. She has been lying all her life, telling stories to people, making up fantasies, and suddenly she comes to a point where that's not enough. All she can do is tell the truth" (qtd in Welch).

8 Both Pullman and Le Guin construct their notions of the afterlife according to what Alan Bernstein calls the "neutral death," a notion of the afterlife where all are treated equally, as distinguished from "moral death," where the dead are punished according to their deserts. At different times and in different sources, one finds examples of both neutral death and moral death in both the Hebrew and the Greek traditions of the afterlife. The Old Testament has two notions of Hell: Sheol—the pit (Vulgate *Infernus* or *abyssus*)—and Ge Hinnom (Vulgate *Gehenna*). Sheol was probably originally a neutral underworld, but came over time to be divided into levels and opposed to Ge-Hinnom, the place of infant sacrifice carried out by the pagans, and thus fittingly symbolic of the punishment to be meted out to those who practiced terrible violence or cruelty (Bernstein 133-202).

9 Le Guin's earliest works set in Earthsea are two short stories published in 1964: "The Word of Unbinding," in which the land of the dead is first introduced, and "The Rule of Names," both available in *The Wind's Twelve Quarters* (1975). Thereafter she published the Earthsea trilogy, which comprises *A Wizard of Earthsea* (1968), *The Tombs of Atuan* (1971), and *The Farthest Shore* (1972), all following the career of the master

magician Ged. Much later she published a fourth Earthsea novel, *Tehanu* (1990). In 2001, she published *Tales from Earthsea*, a collection of stories including "Dragonfly" (originally published in 1997 in *Legends*), which is set in a period of time just before *The Other Wind* and which introduces the character of Irian, who is important to Le Guin's concept of dragons. Studies of Le Guin's mythology in the Earthsea stories and novels can be found in Rochelle and Shippey. Shippey's article contains an interesting analysis of Le Guin's construction of religion and death in the novels of the trilogy. On Le Guin's revision of Earthsea in *Tehanu*, see Hunt and Lenz 68-9.

10 Another aspect of Hell is evoked by Tehanu's burning—the pagan Semitic practice of burning infants as sacrifices to Moloch or Baal at Ge Hinnom (Gehenna). The condemnation of this practice by biblical writers led to the notion of a moral Hell involving "long-lasting fire." See Bernstein 168-69, and my note above.

11 Dragons are extremely important to Le Guin's strongly Jungian notion of the psyche. See also "Myth and Archetype in Science Fiction" 69-70.

12 "The Word of Unbinding" and *The Farthest Shore* have similar stories, both of which are thematically close to *The Other Wind*. In each, a character attempts to escape death by using perverse and destructive magic, and must be hunted down at great cost. Like the Harry Potter stories of J.K. Rowling, these works depict attempts to attain immortality as not just misguided, but evil.

13 Le Guin says: "The trilogy is, in one aspect, about the artist. The artist as magician.... Wizardry is artistry. The trilogy is then, in this sense, about art, the creative experience, the creative process" ("Dreams" 53).

14 According to Shippey, this underworld is neither Christian nor classical but a kind of concrete realization of the loss of faith as experienced during the Victorian era (115).

15 For Pullman's notions of myth, see his *A Word or Two About Myths*.

16 The Harrowing episode in *The Lion, the Witch and the Wardrobe*—the unfreezing of the captives of the White Witch—follows Aslan's sacrifice. This might be classified by Le Guin as an example of "living" myth. Since the concept of frozen captives may be borrowed from the Middle English *Sir Orfeo*, there may also be a distant connection with the Orpheus myth here as well.

WORKS CITED

Bernstein, Alan E. *The Formation of Hell: Death and Retribution in the Ancient and Early Christian Worlds*. Ithaca: Cornell UP, 1993.

Colbert, David. *The Magical Worlds of Phillip Pullman*. London: Puffin, 2006.

Hunt, Peter, and Millicent Lenz. *Alternative Worlds in Fantasy Fiction*. New York: Continuum, 2001.

Le Guin, Ursula. "Myth and Archetype in Science Fiction." *The Language of the Night*. Ed. Susan Wood. New York: Berkley Books, 1979. 73-81.

_____. *The Farthest Shore*. 1972. New York: Bantam, 1975.

_____. *The Other Wind*. New York: Ace Books, 2001.

_____. *Tehanu*. 1990. New York: Simon and Schuster, 2001.

_____. "Why are Americans Afraid of Dragons?" *The Language of the Night*. Ed. Susan Wood. New York: Putnam, 1979. 39-45

_____. *The Wind's Twelve Quarters*. New York: Harper and Row, 1975.

Lenz, Millicent, and Carole Scott, eds. *His Dark Materials Illuminated*. Detroit: Wayne State UP, 2003.

Levenson, Jon D. *Creation and the Persistence of Evil: The Jewish Drama of Divine Omnipotence*. San Francisco: Harper and Row, 1988.

MacCulloch, J.A. *The Harrowing of Hell*. Edinburgh: T & T Clarke, 1930.

Miller, Laura. "Far From Narnia." *The New Yorker* 26 Dec. 2005: 52-75.

Pullman, Phillip. *The Amber Spyglass*. New York: Alfred Knopf, 2000.

_____. *A Word or Two about Myths*. London: Canongate, 2005.

Rochelle, Warren G. *Communities of the Heart*. Liverpool: Liverpool UP, 2001.

Shippey, Thomas. "The Magic Art and Evolution of Words: 'The Earthsea Trilogy.'" *Ursula K. Le Guin*. Ed. Harold Bloom. New York: Chelsea House, 1986. 99-117.

Squires, Claire. *Phillip Pullman, Master Storyteller: A Guide to the Worlds of His Dark Materials*. New York: Continuum, 2006.

Welch, David. "Phillip Pullman Reaches the Garden." Interview. 2000. Accessed 5 August 2008. www.powells.com/authors/pullman.html.

Neomedievalism as Revised Medievalism in *Commedia* Illustrations

Karl Fugelso

Many descriptions of neomedievalism have fit well within the parameters of medievalism,[1] which is defined by *Studies in Medievalism* as "any aspect of the post-medieval idea and study of the Middle Ages and the influence, both scholarly and popular, of this study on Western society after 1500."[2] But I believe that neomedievalism falls outside the spirit, if not the letter, of this slippery definition if we underscore the revisionist implications of "neo"—that is, if we treat neomedievalism as interpretations of interpretations of the Middle Ages. As I hope to demonstrate through questions invited by *Commedia* illustrations, even the slightest possibility of an intermediary between medieval culture and ostensibly direct medievalism raises issues foreign to truly direct medievalism and complicates our field in ways that cast new light on it and on all other investigation into historical referencing. By greatly compounding the potential routes, and perhaps roots, of medieval influence, the mere possibility of a post-medieval intervention underscores the many challenges inherent in determining the genealogy of allusions to the past and in defining the intentions behind those references. It highlights the ambiguities and lacunae in our historical knowledge and reminds us that we can never be completely sure of the past or its motives.[3]

As many scholars have noted, every work of art has an infinite range of possible sources.[4] Indeed, just one category of potential influences on post-medieval illustrations of the *Commedia*, post-medieval texts, is so vast that, beyond perhaps this comment, it cannot be meaningfully summarized here. Moreover, before we can even begin to discuss other post-medieval influences on those illustrations, we must address a wide range of possible medieval influences, including early commentaries on the *Commedia*; other medieval texts; individual medieval images, especially *Commedia* miniatures; widespread medieval motifs and/or tropes; broader principles of medieval art; and medieval culture apart from conventions of text and/or image.

Fortunately, some of these potential medieval sources can be dispatched rather quickly, for they probably did not have any direct impact on post-medieval *Commedia* images. The commentaries, for example, almost certainly had a direct influence on some medieval miniatures, as when the anonymous Sienese illuminator of British Library MS Yates Thompson 36 departed in the early 1440s from Dante and, in depicting not just one but multiple boats ferrying sinners across the Acheron, adhered to the extremely popular mid-fourteenth-century commentary by Andrea di Ser Valle (noted by Brieger 110).[5] And through those miniatures, the commentaries may have had an indirect impact on post-medieval art, as when Botticelli's late fifteenth- or early sixteenth-century drawings of the *Commedia* echo the Yates Thompson miniatures.[6] But to my knowledge, no post-medieval illustration of the *Commedia* directly refers to any aspect of the commentaries that is otherwise unique to those texts, that does not also appear in at least one image pre-dating the illustration in question.

Indeed, to my knowledge, none of the post-medieval *Commedia* illustrations directly refer to any medieval text other than the *Commedia*, and even the latter may not have had a direct influence on some of the illustrations. Many sixteenth-century *Commedia* woodcuts, for instance, are so similar to earlier prints that they almost seem to come from the same blocks.[7] And though no two nineteenth-century engravings of the *Commedia* are quite that similar, many were turned out in such short order and show such strong influences from their predecessors that they at least cast doubt on whether their creators had first-hand knowledge of Dante's text, as Eugene Paul Nassar suggests (19). For example, Yan Dargent's 1879 print of Dante meeting the arch-heretic Farinata in *Inferno* 10 has roughly the same landscape, figural arrangement, viewing angle, scale, and degree of chiaroscuro as Gustave Doré's extremely famous 1861 print of that same episode.[8]

Of course, if artists could not be bothered to read the oft-translated, widely circulated text they were illustrating, they could hardly be expected to track down and study rare images of it. And, indeed, none of the artists who worked on Dante's text after the sixteenth century demonstrates unequivocal knowledge of *Commedia* miniatures, or, for that matter, other particular medieval images. But by the beginning of the Romantic movement in the late eighteenth and early nineteenth century, many *Commedia* illustrators do invoke widespread medieval motifs, such as the ram representing Aries in the sky of Joseph Anton Koch's engraving for *Inferno* 1, and medieval tropes, such as the continuous-narrative format in that illustration and in Koch's drawing of *Inferno* 13.[9] Moreover, many more artists from that point on employ broad principles associated with medieval art, such as the extreme expressionism in Doré's heavily shadowed engraving of Count Ugolino grappling with his hunger in *Inferno* 33 as his offspring wilt at his feet.[10] And few postmedieval artists are immune to other cultural aspects that became closely identified with the Middle Ages—such as the overt piety in Doré's illustration of Dante kneeling with his hands clasped and head bowed as John tests him in *Paradiso* 26.[11]

Of course, these may not be examples of deliberate medievalism, for, as is often the case with ostensible acts of historical referencing, many of these apparent allusions have blurry borders and a questionable provenance. Moreover, many of them may not actually refer to medieval traits but, rather, to traits that have been merely perceived as medieval. Piety and expressionism, for example, hardly seem to be characteristic of the Middle Ages when one looks at *Commedia* miniatures, for many of the latter, such as the depiction of Dante being examined by John in Biblioteca Medicea Laurenziana MS Plutei 40.1, are so stoic as to be thoroughly drained of all feeling, including piety.[12] Indeed, as a stone-faced Dante gazes at John in this miniature while counting on his fingers, and as John points at Dante from beneath a dome of hair that hides everything but his lower limbs and upper face, the image seems rather—and pointedly—pedantic.

But, of course, this example raises another issue that haunts medievalism, namely, how do we define the Middle Ages? Does the fact that the Plutei miniature was executed in 1456 by an Italian contemporary of Leonardo and Donatello qualify it as a Renaissance work? Or are the rules different for manuscripts? What are the artistic common denominators of the Middle Ages, if any, and how are they expressed? Must they have been recognized as such during the Middle Ages themselves? And, if so, in what form must they have been recognized—by texts that explicitly address art, such as Theophilus' *On Divers Arts*? By texts that do not explicitly address art but pertain to fields that were perceived as related to art, such as Scholastic treatises on rhetoric? By instructional images, such as those found in workshop pattern books or in the margins of unfinished manuscripts? Moreover, who is qualified to judge these criteria? Medieval critics? Postmedieval critics?

And where do the medievalist's perceptions of the Middle Ages fit into these definitions? If, as in the case of William Blake, we have verbal testimony from a medievalist as to his or her impressions of the *Commedia*, to what extent should we see his or her illustrations through the lens of that testimony? When Blake says in an inscription on one of his two *c*1824-27 drawings for *Inferno* 4, "Every thing in Dantes Comedia shews That for Tyrannical Purposes he has made This World the Foundation of All & the Goddess Nature & not the Holy Ghost,"[13] to what degree can we read his images as matching that perception? And at what point do his perceptions trump our own reading of his images and perhaps of the Middle Ages? Furthermore, at what point, if any, do the medievalist's perceptions render the medieval evidence itself irrelevant? When Blake says Dante was "an atheist—A mere politician busied about this world," does it matter whether we have medieval testimony to the contrary (qtd. in Bindman 13)?[14] And if so, when does it matter? Moreover, how do we define the medievalist's views with enough confidence to be sure we are, in fact, seeing his or her interpretation of the Middle Ages, rather than our own? When Blake said he began his *Commedia* illustrations with "fear and trembling" and when he then said "you'll do" after the young painter Samuel Palmer said that he, Palmer, had had enough of fear and trembling, what did Blake mean (qtd. in Bindman 7-8)?[15] Was he denigrating the power of the *Commedia*, as Bindman claims (8)? Was he seriously or ironically commenting on Palmer's self-confidence at the ripe old age of nineteen?

And if we cannot be sure what constitutes the Middle Ages or the motivations for an instance of medievalism, how can we trace the medieval sources of that act? Are visual parallels enough, such as the ram in the sky on the opening page of an early fifteenth-century *Inferno* in Rimini Biblioteca Civica Gambalunga MS 4.I.II.25, and the ram in the sky of Koch's engraving for *Inferno* 1?[16] And if so, how many and what type of visual parallels are required for a match, particularly in the case of broad principles associated with medieval art, such as the abstraction in a mid-fourteenth-century Sienese miniature from Perugia Biblioteca Augusta MS L.70, which depicts Dante and the three beasts of *Inferno* 1 repeatedly appearing against the outlines of

blue hills, and in Leonard Baskin's zoological symbol of the Violent Against
Nature for his 1970 cycle of *Inferno* prints? Must these parallels be unique to
the works being compared?[17] What if some of these parallels occur in other
known images that predate the instance of apparent medievalism? What about
the ever-present possibility that there is at least one other, unknown work that
shares these parallels and predates the instance of apparent medievalism? Do
we also need verbal evidence from the medievalist about his or her sources,
as when Koch says he looked to early fourteenth-century Italian frescoes as
a model for his illustrations (Riemann-Reyher 85-90)? Would we need it from
contemporaries of the medievalist, as when Koch's colleagues confirm that
he looked to Italian masters of late medieval art for his models?[18] And, again,
who is to judge the validity of this evidence—the medievalist's contemporaries
or more recent observers?

Of course, these questions do not get any easier when we look at
interpretations of interpretations of the Middle Ages. In fact, they often get
quite a bit harder. Though the Middle Ages, in and of themselves, are no more
difficult to define for neomedievalism than for medievalism, their relationship
to neomedievalism is frequently more complex and/or ambiguous than their
relationship to medievalism, for they often have many more potential paths of
influence. In addition to the possibility that they may affect a neomedievalist work
directly—either in part, or, if the neomedievalism of the work is a misperception,
in full—they may also influence it via a wide range of postmedieval intermediaries,
including texts, images, principles, practices, beliefs, mindsets, and so forth. Thus,
the actual path or paths of influence may be buried beneath a far greater range
of possibilities than is the case with medievalism.

Of course, medieval influence is also more likely to be diluted and/or
distorted as it passes through intermediaries, for with each new interpreter come
additional opportunities for altering a medieval trait and/or its original contexts.
In some cases, these changes would seem to be deliberate, as when, to great
and highly appropriate effect, Rico Lebrun's *Commedia* drawings from 1963
only selectively adhere to Romantic associations of darkness with the Middle
Ages.[19] But in other cases, neomedievalists may not fully realize how they or
their immediate sources depart from their medieval roots, as when Lebrun's
publisher, Baskin, almost drowns the Violent against Nature and some of his
other *Commedia* subjects in darkness.[20]

Indeed, intentionality becomes much more problematic for neomedievalism
than for medievalism, as, by my definition, true neomedievalism comprises
only indirect contact with the Middle Ages. If we have doubts as to whether
medievalists are fully aware of their medieval sources, how can we discern
the degree to which neomedievalists are cognizant of *their* medieval roots,
or, for that matter, their postmedieval roots? Baskin clearly knew Lebrun's
work, but, to my knowledge, he never recorded his thoughts on whether
it affected his own *Commedia* illustrations. Nor, to my knowledge, did he
discuss whether the latter had been affected by other medieval, medievalist,
or neomedievalist works, besides the *Commedia*. So, if we decide a work is

neomedievalist, how can we determine whether or not its creator was aware of being a neomedievalist?

Further, as I asked earlier with regard to the self-consciousness of medievalists as medievalists, does that awareness matter? Does it matter whether and to what degree Baskin knew he was borrowing from Lebrun or other post-medieval sources? Or is our perception of neomedievalism as neomedievalism sufficient? And if so, upon what criteria should we base that judgment, particularly with regard to art? Are parallels in style or content any more or less valid for neomedievalism than for medievalism? Does uniqueness matter any more for neomedievalist parallels than for medievalist parallels? Do we need outside corroboration for our perception of those parallels? And, if so, when, what type, and from whom? Is it sufficient to have verbal testimony by our contemporaries or near contemporaries, as in the many claims over the last twenty-five years that a 1983 illustration by Tom Phillips simulates a comic-book rendering of a Blake illustration for *Inferno* 22?[21] What about visual testimony by contemporaries of the neomedievalist, such as the parallels between Baskin's sketchy, often heavily shaded *Commedia* prints and Barry Moser's sketchy, often heavily shaded *Commedia* drawings?[22] In texts by the neomedievalist, is the defining of sources necessary, as in Phillips' admission that his illustration of *Inferno* 22 is a parody of Blake's (299)? What about some combination thereof? And what role, if any, is played in this identification by the self-awareness, or lack thereof, on the part of medievalists who may have influenced the neomedievalist, by, say, Lebrun's awareness that he is invoking Neogothic precepts that were then adopted from him by Baskin, or Blake's awareness of his medieval departure from optical realism in the illustration parodied by Phillips? To what degree do these and other ambiguities and lacunae of medievalism expand or compound in neomedievalism?

Of course, ultimately, these gaps and grey areas cannot be measured. But there can be little doubt that at least some and perhaps all of them do, in fact, grow during the adaptation of medievalism by neomedievalism, for the role of medievalism in relaying the Middle Ages to neomedievalists compounds the possible routes, and perhaps roots, of medieval influence while sometimes also directly diluting or distorting that influence. This growing obfuscation often makes instances of neomedievalism more difficult to define than instances of medievalism. But contrary to appearances, that is not necessarily a bad thing. Indeed, it may be quite a good thing, for in complicating the genealogy of postmedieval references to the Middle Ages, this obfuscation invites deeper thought on the nature of historical allusions. It challenges the assumptions of all inquiry into how the past has been recycled, revived, revised, and rejected. And it underscores the subtlety and pervasiveness with which the past may endure. Even as it highlights the elusiveness of historical referencing and calls into question our methods of pursuing it, it foregrounds the importance of doing so and confirms the validity of our field.

TOWSON UNIVERSITY

NOTES

1 An earlier version of this paper was delivered on October 5, 2007 at the 22nd Annual International Conference on Medievalism in London, Ontario, where it profited greatly from the dialogue that ensued among many members of the audience. It has also benefited from the extraordinarily attentive comments by the anonymous readers for *The Year's Work in Medievalism*.

2 See the title page of any recent issue of *Studies in Medievalism*.

3 For historical framing of this subjectivity in the context of medieval(ist) studies, see Stock.

4 Of course, by "sources" I and the scholars to whom I refer mean not only earlier works of art, but also all experiences that may have influenced the creator(s) of the work in question.

5 For a reproduction of the miniature, see plate 66b in Volume 2 of Brieger, Meiss, and Singleton.

6 Kenneth Clark makes a case for Botticelli having been influenced by the Yates Thompson miniatures (16).

7 This repetitiveness has been noted by, among others, Eugene Paul Nassar (16).

8 For reproductions of these illustrations, see Nassar (154-55)

9 For reproductions of these illustrations, see Nassar (39, 175).

10 For a reproduction of this illustration, see Nassar (368).

11 For a reproduction of this illustration, see plate 32 in Taylor and Finley.

12 For a reproduction of the Plutei miniature, see plate 500b in Volume 2 of Brieger, Meiss, and Singleton.

13 For a reproduction of the drawing, see figure 7 in Bindman.

14 According to Bindman, Blake made this comment to the journalist Henry Crabb Robinson on December 17, 1825 (8).

15 According to Palmer, Blake made these comments in October 1824.

16 For a reproduction of the miniature, see plate 8b in Volume 2 of Brieger, Meiss, and Singleton. For a reproduction of Koch's image, see page 39 in Nassar, as mentioned above in note 9.

17 For a reproduction of the miniature see color plate II in Volume 2 of Brieger, Meiss, and Singleton. For a reproduction of Baskin's illustration, see plate 51 in Taylor and Finley.

18 See for example an 1805 letter by August Wilhelm Schlegel to Goethe, as noted by Riemann-Reyher (89-90).

19 For the most available reproductions of Lebrun's drawings, see the sample in Taylor and Finley.

20 For a sample of Baskin's *Commedia* drawings, see Taylor and Finley.

21 See, for example, Joachim Möller, "Dante, englisch," in *Dantes Göttliche Komödie*, 153-182 (180). For reproductions of Phillips' and Blake's illustrations, see plates 182 and 183, respectively, in Möller.

22 For reproductions of Moser's illustrations, see Allen Mandelbaum's three-volume translation of the *Divine Comedy*.

WORKS CITED

Bindman, David. *The* Divine Comedy: *William Blake*. Paris: Bibliothèque de l'Image, 2000.

Brieger, Peter. "Pictorial Commentaries to the *Commedia.*" *Illuminated Manuscripts of the* Divine Comedy. Eds. Peter Brieger, Millard Meiss, and Charles S. Singleton. Bollingen Series 81. Vol. 1. Princeton: Princeton UP, 1969. 81-113.

Brieger, Peter, Millard Meiss, and Charles S. Singleton, eds. *Illuminated Manuscripts of the* Divine Comedy. Bollingen Series 81. 2 Vols. Princeton: Princeton UP, 1969.

Clark, Kenneth. *The Drawings by Sandro Botticelli for Dante's* Divine Comedy. New York: Harper & Row, 1976.

Mandelbaum, Allen, trans. *Divine Comedy.* By Dante Alighieri. New York: Bantam, 1980-82.

Nassar, Eugene Paul. *Illustrations to Dante's* Inferno. Rutherford: Fairleigh Dickinson UP, 1994.

Phillips, Tom, trans. and illus. *Dante's* Inferno. New York and London: Thames & Hudson, 1985.

Riemann-Reyher, Marie Ursula. "Dantes Traum der Läuterung—Brücke zwischen Klassizismus und Romantik." *Dantes* Göttliche Komödie*: Drucke und Illustrationen aus Sechs Jahrhunderten.* Ed. Lutz S. Malke. Berlin: Staatliche Museen zu Berlin, 2000. 81-108.

Stock, Brian. "Romantic Attitudes and Academic Medievalism." *Listening for the Text: On the Uses of the Past.* Baltimore and London: The Johns Hopkins UP, 1990. 52-74.

Taylor, Charles H. and Patricia Finley, *Images of the Journey in Dante's* Divine Comedy. New Haven and London: Yale UP, 1997.

Is Orientalism Medievalism? Or, Edward Said, Are You a Saracen?

William Calin

It will come as no surprise that postcolonialism and orientalism, like so many other approaches, once they are legitimized, may be deemed chic and cutting-edge and, consequently, will be adopted by specialists in other fields. For example, we find interesting new work in the Middle Ages and the Renaissance from a consciously postcolonial perspective, although significantly more prevalent in English and Spanish studies than in French, German, and Italian.[1] Postcolonial theory is or can be applied to the crusades and the conquest of the New World, relations between Christian Europe and the Muslim East, the conquest of England by the French in 1066, and the attitudes of Christian Europe toward its religious or ethnic minorities.

Such work has the advantages and disadvantages that one can imagine. It opens the field to a new vision and asks new questions about our canonical texts or uncovers hitherto neglected texts. And it can be made manifest in a simplistic, derivative, cliché-ridden rhetoric by people lacking both historical and literary sensitivity. Not to speak of ritual denunciations of the empowered, and the sentimental fetishization of the disempowered.

Another area, one in which I have been engaged personally, is the literature of the French provinces or regions and, more specifically, those having an autonomous cultural tradition because embodied in a language other than French. In the United States we are only beginning to explore this domain. I should mention my book *Minority Literatures and Modernism*; postcolonialism is one approach among many in a work concerned with the practical criticism and periodization of the modern literatures in Breton, Occitan, and Lowland Scots. As it turns out, medievalism plays a part in the twentieth-century minority literatures. The writers and the political militants seek to reclaim their cultural as well as political history, and they create cultural myths in order to do so. One such myth states that the Middle Ages is quintessentially Occitan/Breton/Scots, that the regional culture enjoyed a rich flowering back then, and that, because of invasion and subjugation by the colonial power in Paris or London, all changed for the worse, ending in something like cultural genocide. The recommendation for contemporary writers is to turn to inspiration from the Middle Ages—the period's writers and books.

In his book of the same name, Edward Said wrote brilliantly on the phenomenon of Orientalism, a doctrine or, more accurately, a habit of thought or mentality, held consciously or unconsciously, by writers and scholars alike, since the second half of the eighteenth century. This is the mentality according to which the Orient (in Said's case, the Muslim Arab Orient) is envisaged as a threatening entity on which are displaced a host of elements that attract and repel the West. These include, among others, riches, luxury, sensuality, immorality, and decadence.

According to Said, the Orient is a source, rival, and image of the Other that helps define Europe. Orientalism is a discourse about the Orient which offers a means of structuring and dominating the Orient. Although the Orient exists in its own reality, we create it for ourselves in a relationship of power and hegemony, our conception of it being both political and cultural. In other words, our Orientalist mindset is never the truth but rather a series of representations from the outside by Europeans for Europeans: Orientalism is to be found at the intersection of society, history, and textuality, and of ideology, politics, and power. Above all, the Orient is always conceived as alterity, as the opposite of (or, occasionally, the same as) us in structures of bipolarity created by us in our image, always the Other and the object seen from the perspective of the Self and the subject.

Among the writers scrutinized in depth by Said we find Richard Burton, François-René de Chateaubriand, Gustave Flaubert, Gérard de Nerval, and Ernest Renan. I leave out the "pure scholars," who are of less interest for this paper. From my own reading, I am especially cognizant of the sexual element in Orientalism. For example, the acme of Flaubert's sexual existence was the night he spent with a famous Egyptian courtesan, an experience he treasured above all others in spite of the bedbugs and the subsequent venereal disease. André Gide, whom Said neglects, discovered his sexuality through boys in Algeria, who initiated him and to whom he returned as frequently as his life permitted.

A secondary topic in Said's masterwork—which he developed further in his *Culture and Imperialism* of 1993—concerns the imperialist experience at the heart of Western culture and history. According to Said, the reality of empire functions as a veiled subtext in Western literature in much the same way as black slavery does in American literature. In addition, given that the imperial impulse gave rise to a flourishing modern economy in the West and that it contributed to the rise of the bourgeoisie, imperialism is also connected to the birth and growth of the pre-eminent bourgeois genre, the modern novel. Examples are Said's own reading of Jane Austen's *Mansfield Park* with the social economy of Sir Bertram's great house derived from the repressive political economy of his plantation in Antigua, or Gayatri Chakravorty Spivak's reading of Charlotte Brontë's *Jane Eyre* where Jane's triumphant emergence is posited upon the degraded occulting of Rochester's wife, a white Creole from the Indies treated as a colonized female subject.

Although I criticize Edward Said for distorting on occasion the page he cites for analysis and for being too hard on the Orientalist scholars, I am of the opinion that Said is one of the great intellectuals of our time, that his contribution to the study of literature and to the history of cultures is deservedly famous, and that his approach and his insights will endure. While agreeing wholeheartedly with so much of his analysis, nevertheless I believe that Said erred by situating the phenomena of Orientalism and of imperialism as connected to the rise of the novel in the eighteenth and nineteenth centuries; or, rather, of implicitly limiting these phenomena to the modern age. I propose that the Saidian schemata came into existence long before the eighteenth century—that is, in the early Middle Ages with the first French *chansons de geste* and *romans courtois*.

Take the case of the *Chanson de Roland*. The Saracens are portrayed as a gathering of fierce, threatening adversaries.[2] Their hordes come from the far corners of the earth—from Cadiz to Kiev, from Ireland to Armenia. They include exotic creatures: the Micenes, pig-people with spines down their backs; the tribe from *Occiant le desert* whose skin is as hard as iron, so that they fight without defensive armour; and the giants of Malprose. Their leaders' names, studded with occlusives and fricatives, create an aura of mystery and horror: Cornablix, Malprimis de Brigal, Escremiz de Valterne, Chernubles de Muneigre, Aelroth, Malquiant, and others. And, in battle,

Cil d'Ociant i braient e henissent,

Arguille si cume chen i glatissent.

(The men of Occiant bray and whinny,

The men of Argoille yelp like dogs.) (vv. 3526-27)

At the same time the Saracens possess untold riches and luxury, including the exotic. They hope to bribe the Franks into leaving by the offer of bears, lions, and greyhounds, seven hundred camels and one thousand falcons, four hundred mules plus fifty carts all bearing Arabian gold. Along with the riches and luxury, as if bound to them and inherent in the people, is treachery, the willingness to trick, lie, and betray.

The opposition of the Self and the Other is absolute:

"Paien unt tort e chrestien unt dreit."

"Nos avum dreit, mais cis glutun unt tort."

(Pagans are in the wrong and Christians are in the right.

We are in the right and these wretches are in the wrong.[3]) (vv. 1015, 1212)

The Frankish response comes in part from the Old Testament: convert or die, and the Saracens all are exterminated except for the queen and her retinue.

The same ethos pervades quite a few other *chansons de geste*. In *Aspremont* and a fair number of texts from the Guillaume Cycle immense hordes of Saracens invade Carolingian Europe, mostly in the south of France but also in Italy. Like Roland, great heroes such as Guillaume's nephew Vivien fall in battle against overwhelming odds. Like Charlemagne, others—Guillaume himself and his forebears—hold out with success. In the epics of revolt it can occur that the rebel hero—Girard de Roussillon or Renaud de Montauban—undertakes a pilgrimage to the Holy Land, which always ends in a crusade, as the near-last stage of repentance and reassimilation into society.

Of course, there is the occasional good Saracen, such as Fierabras or Rainouart, who convert to Christianity and serve the true faith loyally. And there are the Saracen women. In what we can envisage as an adolescent wish-fulfillment phantasm, the Saracen princess, extraordinarily beautiful and passionate yet still a virgin, falls in love with the French hero captured by her father. She lusts after his body and will do anything to have him. The hero insists that she liberate him from prison, help him destroy her father, and return with him to France for conversion and Christian marriage. Of course, she accepts with joy. The road of the sexual is not all that long from, say, *Huon de Bordeaux* to Flaubert, Pierre Loti, and Gide.

In the *roman courtois*—what we call Arthurian romance and the French call *roman breton*—the threatening Other is displaced onto the Celtic Otherworld, which can be found in dreadful lands across the seas (Ireland) or in the *forest aventureuse* (the deep, dark woods) not far from home. The Celtic Orient, as with the Saracen, offers men to be slain and women to be married. The men are ogres or giants, and in romance single combat replaces the pitched battle of *chanson de geste*. The women are, as in the *chanson de geste*, either widows whom the protagonists (Yvain, Guillaume d'Orange) wed after having slain their husbands, or ravishing virgins. This is the pattern in Chrétien de Troyes and his successors, including the great *Lancelot-Grail Cycle*.

In *Le Roman de Tristan*, Tristan conquers monsters in Ireland and eventually brings back with him Isolt. An Irish witch, like her mother, the magnificently manipulative Isolt offers him the gifts of love and death. In the *Prose Lancelot* a good prince from afar, Galehaut (whose mother is a giant) becomes Lancelot's doting and faithful friend. When a rumour is spread that Lancelot has perished, Guinevere grieves but Galehaut dies of chagrin. The homoerotic overtones would have been obvious to the medieval public even though they remained opaque to modern bourgeois scholars. We find, thus, as with the *chanson de geste*, an Other which is threatening, desirable, quasi-magical, and also deceptive, treacherous, and decadent.

This is not to say that the Celtic alterity is identical to the Saracen alterity. They differ, just as the *chanson de geste* as a genre differs from the *roman courtois* as a genre. Nor was there, during the early Middle Ages, anything in fact like an Oriental essence, whether Saracen or Celtic. However, the essence exists in the literature. The literature reflects and helps construct the *mentalités* (mindsets, mental structures) that were as pervasive in the twelfth and thirteenth centuries as in the nineteenth and twentieth. The *trouvères* and their public displaced onto their essentialized Others so much that was desirable and threatening, just as more recent writers and scholars have done.

If my analysis is accurate, the first genuinely modern book would then be Marco Polo's *Le Devisament dou monde* (early fourteenth century), an account of the Orient which, for all its exaggeration and distortion, claims to be and in fact is grounded in identifiable personal experience, a claim to observable reality, and which does treat the Orient from a more pragmatic vantage point.[4]

What conclusions can be drawn from the preceding material? If I am right, we are dealing with archetypal patterns that traverse literary generations and centuries. An Oriental alterity did contribute to the creation of the novel, but it was the novel from the twelfth and thirteenth centuries. Perhaps a challenging, hostile Other is necessary for the rise of civilization and of national cultures—this going back to the Greeks and the Trojans. Perhaps Turkey will never be admitted to the European Union.

One thing is certain, I believe: because of the archetypes, because of their universality, we must never think less of the great medieval and Renaissance books; we must avoid a "reading for evil," both simplistic and reductionist. As Said himself proclaims so eloquently: "Understanding that connection [to imperialism] does not reduce or diminish the novels' value as works of art: on the contrary, because of their *worldliness*, because of their complex affiliations with their real setting, they are more interesting and more valuable as works of art" (*Culture* 13).

Finally, modern Orientalism and modern imperialism came into existence at about the time of the inception of romanticism. I subscribe to Leslie Workman's genial thesis that medievalism is to be found at the heart of romanticism. To a great extent, because of romanticism, medievalism has replaced classicism for large swaths of our modernity. I should also note that the romantics developed their Orientalism in part stimulated by the medieval texts that were being rediscovered. Therefore, modern Orientalism can be considered a phenomenon relating to medievalism and not at all to classicism, content with Greece, Rome, and France, and fearful of intellectual and aesthetic innovation. I add the hope and the expectation that twenty-first century scholarly medievalism and Orientalism will avoid the pitfalls of the past and serve to enrich our culture, to expand our horizons in space and time in order to (I adapt a Crusade slogan), *exalter sainte civilisation.*

UNIVERSITY OF FLORIDA

NOTES

1 In addition to a host of separate articles, see the important collections by Cohen, and Ingham and Warren; also the volume by Ganim.

2 On the Saracens and *chanson de geste*, see Bancourt and Daniel.

3 A more vivid translation could go like this: "Pagans are wrong and Christians are right. / We are right and these bastards are wrong."

4 I use the edition by Ménard et al.; five volumes have been published as of September 2007.

WORKS CITED

Bancourt, Paul. *Les Musulmans dans les chansons de geste du cycle du roi.* 2 vols. Aix-en-Provence: Publications de l'Université de Provence, 1982.

Brault, Gerard J., ed. *The Song of Roland: An Analytical Edition.* 2 vols. University Park: Pennsylvania State UP, 1978.

Cohen, Jeffrey Jerome, ed. *The Postcolonial Middle Ages.* New York: St. Martin's Press, 2000.

Calin, William. *Minority Literatures and Modernism: Scots, Breton, and Occitan, 1920-1990.* Toronto: University of Toronto Press, 2000.

Daniel, Norman. *Heroes and Saracens: An Interpretation of the* Chansons de Geste. Edinburgh: Edinburgh UP, 1984.

Ganim, John M. *Medievalism and Orientalism*. New York: Palgrave Macmillan, 2005.

Ingham, Patricia Clare, and Michelle R. Warren, eds. *Postcolonial Moves: Medieval Through Modern*. New York: Palgrave Macmillan, 2003.

Polo, Marco. *Le Devisement du monde*. Eds. Philippe Ménard et al. Geneva: Droz, 2001– .

Said, Edward W. *Culture and Imperialism*. New York: Knopf, 1993.

_____. "Jane Austen and Empire." *Culture and Imperialism*. 95-116.

_____. *Orientalism*. New York: Pantheon Books, 1978.

Spivak, Gayatri Chakravorty. "Three Women's Texts and a Critique of Imperialism." *Critical Inquiry* 12 (1985-86): 243-61. Rep. in *A Critique of Postcolonial Reason: Toward a History of the Vanishing Present*. Cambridge, MA: Harvard UP, 1999. 112-40.

Workman, Leslie J. "Medievalism and Romanticism." *Poetica* 39-40 (1994): 1-44.

_____. "Medievalism and Romantic Scholarship." *The Round Table* 7 (March (March 1992): 1-23.

On the Threshold:
The Liminal Self in the Twelfth and Twentieth Centuries

Jonathan Rollins

The traditional humanist conception of the self as an autonomous, unified subject has been a central feature of modernity in the West since the end of the Middle Ages. For centuries, this ideal modern self has (in theory, at least) functioned as the subject of its own narrative universe, asserting its will and dominating through power and knowledge the objects and others it has encountered. However, significant changes to this model begin to occur in the nineteenth century and continue in earnest through the twentieth and into the twenty-first. These changes/crises constitute a critique of what is often called the modern (Renaissance) humanist self–the *res cogitans* or thinking thing. Through a sort of reverse symmetry, the unravelling post-humanist self of the late twentieth and early twenty-first centuries bears striking similarities to the newly emerging pre-modern or proto-modern individual of the twelfth century. Is this apparent diachronic symmetry of the self part of a more general late twentieth-century "return of the Middle Ages" (to use a phrase made famous by Umberto Eco)? Are we, as has been suggested, on the verge of a New Middle Ages? That might be overstating the case: we do not seem to be in the midst of a de-evolution or wholesale jettisoning of modernity. Nevertheless, in the evolution of the self, certain key elements of premodernity resurface in postmodernity.

The potential list of works relevant to the support of such an hypothesis is an extremely long one. These texts articulate a comparably liminal selfhood through a variety of discursive practices that traverse the generic spectrum from the (auto)biographical to the fictional. For practical reasons, it is not possible to give detailed consideration to each of them here. Therefore, for the sake of brevity, I will focus on a comparison of two works that narrate a similar version of the self: *Monodiae* or *De vita sua, sive monodiarum libri tres* (translated by Benton as "Memoirs"),[1] an "autobiographical" text by Guibert de Nogent (1064-c.1125),[2] and Salman Rushdie's novel *Midnight's Children* (published in 1981). Both provide significant contributions in their respective periods to the textual evolution of a self that is fragmented, plural, hybrid, decentred, and liminal (though not exclusively autobiographical), and that emerges in the margins of the so-called modern, humanist self.

In suggesting a link between the twelfth century and the contemporary West, I build on a critical foundation laid by others who have compared these two periods. Colin Morris, for example, suggests in *The Discovery of the Individual: 1050-1200* that there are points of contact between the High Middle Ages and the late twentieth century (163):

> Our connection with the age of Abelard, then, is partly continuous,
> partly a question of loss and recovery. It is also perhaps true that
> we have with it a special sympathy of our own. Then, as now, men

faced a crisis of identity. They found themselves in a rapidly changing society, whose stock of knowledge was increasing at a speed which made it difficult to *digest*....Aelred and his older contemporaries stood at the beginning of a long history which is just ending, creators of that Western Christendom of whose dissolution we are the witnesses. It is perhaps natural that the same fundamental questions have posed themselves again about our identity as individuals and our function in the world (166-7).

It is significant that Morris draws a connection between these diachronic similarities and the idea of a crisis of identity in both periods. Thus, in the development of this argument, I am not alone in turning to the medieval past as a means to interpret contemporary culture. Nor am I alone in recycling the Middle Ages.

The critical genealogy for this project stretches back to the early twentieth century. In 1919, at the end of the Great War and in the midst of social and political turmoil in Russia, Nikolai Berdiaev declares that the Renaissance is over (16). Five years later in Berlin, he declares the advent of a "New Middle Ages" (17), which he characterizes as the end of humanism, of individualism, and of liberalism (72). In the 1970s, Umberto Eco observes that the "Return of the Middle Ages" has become an obsession not only of academic round tables and high-brow *literati* but also of popular culture and the popular media (63). Eco's interest can be summarized by his claim that "all the problems of the Western world emerged in the Middle Ages" and, therefore, an examination of the Middle Ages "means looking at our infancy" (64-5). He argues that there are important parallels between "certain moments and situations" of that other, re-imagined period and the present (74).

Alain Minc, another recycler of the Middle Ages, pays homage to Berdiaev in the title of his own work, *Le nouveau Moyen Âge*, or *The New Middle Ages*, published in 1993. Minc indicates that while things have changed since Berdiaev first hypothesized the end of the Renaissance or modernity (most notably with the collapse of the Soviet Empire, which Minc claims was an event even more cataclysmic than the fall of Rome), we are, indeed, in a new Middle Age. He insists that this new era is characterized by the disappearance of "centre" and the development of "grey zones" that multiply beyond all authority. I would contend that these grey zones, presented under the rubric of hybridity and liminality–and more specifically the liminal self, are vital to the convincing development of such a diachronic argument. Minc suggests that the present is an age in which reason is effaced as a founding principle and replaced by ideology and superstition. In these new Middle Ages, the crises and spasms that are the everyday adornments of the world constitute a revolutionary challenge to the modern Cartesian subject (10-11). While Minc's argument is valid, it is not entirely free from millennial anxiety. He concludes his comparison of the old Middle Ages and the new with the following question: *après la grande peur de l'an 1000, le désarroi de l'an 2000?* "After the great fear of the year 1000, the disarray of the year 2000?" (11). I wish to pull back from the panic in order to present these so-called new Middle Ages in a more positive light; that is, to see the flux, the loss of centre, and the aleatory nature of this new age as an opportunity to rethink some of the problems or baggage inherited from the modern age.

To a certain extent, I concur with Mikhail Epstein in his association of the postmodern with the medieval. Yet, it is important to stipulate that what is occurring is not a simple return to the old but a *parody* that repeats aspects of the original Middle Ages with critical differences.[3] Despite his unequivocal dicta, even Berdiaev seems willing to grant that there is no going back to old hierarchies or power structures (73). The significance of Epstein's argument is that it makes a distinction between the extended new Middle Ages, which he refers to as postmodernity, and that relatively brief period of transition between modernity and postmodernity, which he calls postmodernism. My argument regarding the twelfth and twentieth centuries rests on this idea of liminality. I won't attempt to argue, as does Epstein, that postmodernity (or his own version of it) is analogous to the Middle Ages as a whole; I find it too problematic to attempt to reconcile these two ages on such a general level. Instead, I argue that the liminality of the twelfth century with regard to nascent modernity is analogous to the liminality of the late twentieth and early twenty-first centuries as it pertains to the waning of that modernity (late modernity, that is, in an altered or developed form). Thus, building on a foundation laid, in part, by Berdiaev, Eco, Epstein, Morris, and others who, like R. Howard Bloch, insist that "The institutional signs of a New Medievalism are everywhere," I also argue that there are important diachronic similarities and relationships (67). However, my interest is somewhat more narrowly focused. This study concentrates on the concept of the individual, the self, or the problematic "I" and examines how that liminal self is configured as a decentred *other-among-others* in these two seemingly different yet similarly transitional periods, rather than attempting to argue for a more general, postmodern new medievalism.[4]

One important question that this hypothesis raises is "Why the twelfth century?" Eco's interest in the Middle Ages, for example, spanned the entire period from the decline of the Roman Empire to the rise of the Italian Renaissance. By contrast, my much narrower interest lies in that period of cultural and intellectual expansion commonly (although not unproblematically) referred to as "the twelfth-century renaissance."[5] While one might be hard-pressed to argue that there are significant similarities between Beowulf and Virginia Woolf (or Christa Woolf, to move the comparison farther along), one can argue that the issues and anxieties attendant upon the emergent modern self of many twelfth-century texts anticipate the corresponding issues and anxieties of the waning of that modern, humanist self in the twentieth century. The latter is an inclusive repetition of the former–inclusive in that it repeats the medieval without completely excluding the complex development of the various "humanisms" and modernities of the intervening period. I do not espouse the millennialist postmodern view proposed by Hans Bertens, who claims: "Postmodernity restores to us the world in its pristine indeterminacy."[6]

Yes, postmodernity restores indeterminacy, but it is hardly "pristine." There is no going back to Eden. Thus, postmodernity may be called a parody of the medieval and of humanism insofar as it repeats with critical differences many aspects of both.

The critique or dissolution of "the self as autonomous subject" (Foucault 42) in the twentieth century resonates with the pre-humanist concepts of subjectivity. In order to highlight this correspondence, I have chosen to focus attention on textual selves from opposite ends of humanist modernity in order to explore characteristics common to these two discrete cultural temporalities. However, the fact that one of these texts is generally labelled autobiography and the other historiographic metafiction might lead one to question whether this were not a case of comparing apples to oranges. However, Philippe Lejeune defines autobiography as an objective, factual, sustained focus on the life and development of the individual, governed by the "autobiographical pact," which stipulates a narrative unity between author and subject (14, 19-20), and Karl Joachim Weintraub argues that it is not fully developed in the West until late in the eighteenth century (26). This unified, self-contained version of autobiography will flourish for less than two centuries before evolving into an approach with discursive hybridity and the decentring of its subject self. In fact, it becomes something akin to Guibert de Nogent's text. That is to say, autobiography will become increasingly problematized as the twentieth century progresses. Thus, while Guibert's *De vita sua* is read here as autobiographical, it cannot be contained or accounted for within the limits of that genre as defined by Lejeune. It is a tripartite work in which Guibert, the autobiographical subject, discusses his own moral depravity in the first chapter, then shifts to a general history of his abbey (and its morally suspect population) in the second, and then shifts again to a brief history of a peasant uprising in the Northern French town of Laon (close to Nogent), along with a number of sensational anecdotal accounts of moral depravity, in the third.

Salman Rushdie's *Midnight's Children* similarly blurs those same limits of autobiography but from the opposite direction by presenting a "fluid interplay of history and fiction" in which the fictional self is "dressed in the discursive drag of autobiography" (Hutcheon 1988: 5). His autofictional protagonist, Saleem Sinai (born at the exact moment when India becomes an independent nation), begins his self-narrative with a conventionally autobiographical detail of his birth: "I was born in the city of Bombay." Yet, that convention is immediately undermined as he adds to it the phrase "once upon a time" (9). That mix of autobiography and fairy tale in the first line marks this life story as a discursive hybrid. The further the story progresses, the more the self is decentred from its own hybrid narrative. Like Guibert, Rushdie shifts focus to other stories and histories (others' stories) that test and transgress the boundaries between fact and fiction and, thus, render to the autobiographical (or autofictional) subject an other-among-others.

Hutcheon refers to this sort of hybridity as the "contradictory contamination" or confusion of generic and discursive boundaries between the "self-consciously literary" and the "verifiable historical" that is one aspect of the postmodern in general and of postmodern autobiography in particular. In the "Book of the Self" section of his counter-autobiographical or autofictional *Roland Barthes par Roland Barthes*, Barthes similarly insists, *Tout ceci doit être considéré comme dit par un personnage de roman–ou plutôt par plusieurs* "All of this should be considered as if spoken by a character in a novel–or rather by many" (123). Such discursive hybridity, Hutcheon argues, "challenges the borders we accept as existing between literature and the extra-literary narrative discourses which surround it: history, biography, autobiography" (Hutcheon 224). The "it" to which Hutcheon refers is historiographic metafiction, or that particular form of the postmodern novel (of which she cites Rushdie's *Midnight's Children* as a prime example) that constitutes a discursive hybridity of literature, history, and theory as well as a self-reflexive recognition of both fiction and history as human constructs (5). It is this hybridity in both *De vita sua* and *Midnight's Children* that renders these narratives compatible, comparable representations of the liminal self.

Notwithstanding the counterarguments, Guibert's *De vita sua* (c.1114/17) is traditionally thought of as the first significant "autobiography" after Augustine's *Confessiones*.[7] Like Abelard's autobiographical *Historia calamitatum* written two decades later, *De vita sua* examines in detail the "humanism and subjectivity" of twelfth-century narrative and its "new concern with the experience of the individual" (Wetherbee 127). Having begun his text with the Augustinian *Confiteor...*, Guibert establishes an immediate association between his own confession and that canonical autobiographic confession of his generic predecessor. His object is purportedly self-knowledge:

> dignum ac singulariter salutare est, ut obscuritas rationis meae, per hujusmodi confessiones, crebra tui luminis inquisitione tergatur, quo stabiliter illustrata nunquam dehinceps a se nesciatur.
> It is a worthy act and singularly for my soul's good that through these confessions the darkness of my understanding should be dispersed by the searching rays Thy light often casts upon it, by which, being lastingly illuminated, it may forever know itself. (Nogent 7-8, Benton 37)

However, unlike Augustine, he seems either unwilling or unable to maintain a sustained focus on himself throughout his nominal autobiography, and his memoir wanders away from self (his, at least) rather decisively in the second and third books. The result is a decentring (and, at times, the outright exclusion) of his self in a text in which that self-as-subject ought logically to be the centre. One can only speculate that perhaps after placing himself squarely in the glaring and unbearable light of divine scrutiny, Guibert, a self-proclaimed repeat offender, finds his initial subject-position untenable. The speed with which he shrinks from his own confession and transfers the attention to other sinners and their collective catalogue of depravity suggests that he felt himself an unworthy subject.

The interstitial anxiety produced by straddling intellectual cultures and the moral polarity of good and evil in *De vita sua* finds its counterpart in the anxieties produced by the straddling of national, cultural, linguistic, social, and various other types of boundaries in Rushdie's *Midnight's Children*. Rushdie calls this the "two othernesses" or the "double unbelonging" of the transnational, transcultural hybrid self who finds him- or herself "between here-and-there" (*East, West* 141). Both Rushdie and Guibert use text to write out or confess these anxieties. Through his confessional agonizing, Guibert seems to have found a home (though certainly not a comfortable one) in the liminal space between good and evil, between conversion and perversion, and between different discursive practices (the historical, the autobiographical, the fantastic, the miraculous). In its various interstitialities, the self that he presents has much in common with the decentred liminal subjectivity of twentieth-century theory.

Like Rushdie, Guibert quickly establishes focus on boundaries and the body as central to his articulation of selfhood. Early in *De vita sua*, Guibert de Nogent recounts the derogatory musings of a woman on the day of his baptism:

> Ea ipsa die, dum salutifero fonti inferrer, mulier quaedam–quod mihi puero et jam adolescenti saepenumero joci causa relatum est–de manu rotabat in manum me transferens. "Hunccine," aiebat, "victurum putatis, quem prope natura deficens emembrem edidit, et magis lineamenti quid simile quam corpus dedit?"

> On the very day when I was put into the baptismal font–as I was so often told as a joke in boyhood and even in youth–a certain woman tossed me from hand to hand. "Look at this thing," she said. "Do you think such a child can live, whom nature by a mistake has made almost without limbs, *giving him something more like an outline than a body?*" (Nogent 18-19, Benton 42, my emphasis)

His allegedly shapeless body is here presented in terms of its boundary –not a thing but the outline (the "edge" or *lineamentum*) of a thing. Guibert's description of his birth contributes to this emphasis on the boundary in that he vacillates between life and death, subject and object, and between first- and third-person narration.[8] It is as though he were uncertain as to which side of the frontier to occupy, and so, occupies both:

> Nec mora languidulum quiddam instar abortionis effunditur et, quod fusum erat ad tempus, ut par erat abjectissimo, de absoluta solum matre gaudetur. Erat illius homunculi recens editi adeo miseranda exilitas, ut cadaveruli extemporaliter nati species putaretur.

> At once a weak little being, almost an abortion, was born, and at that timely birth there was rejoicing only for my mother's deliverance, the child being such a miserable object. In that poor mite just born, there was such a pitiful meagreness that he had the corpse-like look of a premature baby. (Nogent 18, Benton 42)

What is remarkable is what Guibert subsequently confesses: *Quae omnia, creator meus, hujus mei, quo vivere videor, status portenta fuere* "All these things, my Creator, were signs of the state in which I seem now to live" (Nogent 20,

Benton 42). These episodes, with their focus on border-crossing, are established as a template for his life, the story of which is presented as a cautionary tale rather than exemplary model designed for emulation.

While the insinuation at the baptismal font cannot be taken literally–Guibert most certainly does have a well-defined body that survives and thrives –this episode is significant for its prophetic and symbolic qualities. That initial state of body-as-outline, the subject of a joke in his early life, has become the defining characteristic of his adult life. That which he presents in his text is not so much his own physical body as its effects–that is to say, the manner in which his body meets, interacts with, or comes into conflict with what is beyond it. Accordingly, he begins his autobiographical text: *Confiteor pueritiae ac juventutis meae mala, adhuc etiam in matura hac aetate aestuantia, et inveterata pravitatum studia, necdum sub defatigati corporis torpore cessantia* "I confess the wickedness I did in childhood and in youth, wickedness that yet boils up in my mature years, and my ingrained love of crookedness, which still lives on in the sluggishness of my worn body" (Nogent 2, Benton 35). Guibert's body-as-limit functions as the locus of what he feels is his unique, perverse, and liminal selfhood.

Rushdie's Saleem Sinai confesses a similar corporeal perversity. Like Guibert's, his physical *corpus* "was to show a marked preference for the impure" rendering him "a misfit" in his own estimation (310). Meanwhile, his written body or textual *corpus*, again like Guibert's, manifests a tendency for discursive perversion, that is, a wandering away from the subject self in a self-narrative and a demonstrated love of "crookedness" as a narrative strategy.[9] Saleem's predilection for tangential wandering is a constant source of frustration for his interlocutor, Padma, and she insists repeatedly that he return to and stick to the point. Of course, he disobeys her directives and deviates from that straight path. In similar fashion, Guibert (who has also disobeyed and habitually strayed from the "straight path") tells us his life story by means of a narrative that wanders to and from the self: now clearly autobiographical, now largely a general history of Laon, now a recounting of generic cautionary tales of specious authenticity and sensational or salacious content. Yet, neither *corpus* is as anomalous as its author imagines it to be. Corresponding representations of the self in the late twentieth and early twenty-first centuries are numerous: Anne Carson's *Autobiography of Red* (1998), Jeffrey Eugenides' *Middlesex* (2003), and Yann Martel's *Self* (1996), among many others. In the twelfth century's literature of the self (autobiographical or otherwise), Abelard and the Archpoet offer similar accounts of the body as the point of departure for what develops into a "poetics of perversion." Here, I am playing with the title of John Freccero's work, *Dante: The Poetics of Conversion*, and with the idea that if conversion is the birth of the "new man" and a turning toward God, then perversion is the re-birth of or reversion to the "old man" in a turning away from God and a disruption of that new, converted self (Freccero 4). In this sense, perversion is the parodic image of conversion.

In the genre of confession or spiritual autobiography, the threshold between the "old man" and the "new man" is the space of conversion (Freccero 25). In textual accounts of conversion, the passage through this threshold produces a split subject or a "radical division between the protagonist and the author who tells his story" (25). Freccero, of course, is not the first to articulate this old/new dichotomy. The division of old and new is a chief feature of Augustine's conversion narrative. Guibert follows the model of Augustine's confession but omits the commitment to a final conversion. He expands or re-enacts the space of confession by making it a serial necessity. Accordingly, the text becomes obsessed with the process of conversion (and re-conversion) without committing to a stable, converted subject position. Guibert seems never to realize "once and for all" the new self of the penitent convert. Instead, he wanders back and forth across the threshold between his old carnal self and the promise of a new, sanctified self, making a place for himself in that in-between space as an unstable self–part penitent, part sinner. The perverse narratives of Guibert and of Rushdie's Saleem Sinai, like that of Calliope Stephanides (the hermaphrodite or "intersexual" protagonist of Eugenides' *Middlesex*), offer a serially multiplying subject and a confusion of the old and the new "man," since the boundary between the two (the conversion/perversion limen) is crossed and then re-crossed or transgressed as a kind of revolving-door threshold.

Rushdie narrates this same wandering, fragmented, liminal self in *Midnight's Children*, a text that is, like *De vita sua*, fascinated with yet also troubled by the idea of disintegration. It is a "journey from wholeness to fragments" (Syed 103). Like Guibert's narrative, Saleem's is splintered. He claims, "I make no comment; these events, which have tumbled from my lips any old how, garbled by haste and emotion, are for others to judge"(30). The implication is that he is assembling a haphazard collage of events (fragments) without the traditional "glue" of a metanarrative. The result, to quote Stock's description of *De vita sua*, is a cubist portrait of the self achieved through a "piling up of different events which seem to him to have the same emotional weight" (506). Whereas in *De vita sua* there is fragmentation of the individual body (in the various accounts of torture and mutilation included in Book Three) as well as crisis in the body politic (illustrated by the uprising at Laon), in Rushdie there is corresponding micro- and macrocosmic disintegration of nations, of cities, families, identities, and bodies. The physical fragmentation of Saleem Sinai's body through a number of accidents or crises is accompanied by a parallel political disintegration of India through the partition that precedes independence, and of Pakistan as its two wings engage in civil war. Where Guibert's self-narrative emphasizes the importance of the *lineamentum* in a corporeal sense, Rushdie reiterates that obsession over bodily boundaries and adds to it a parallel concern with national borders and other limits. Furthermore, he oversteps the boundaries of what is "permitted to do or know or be" and, like Guibert, suffers the consequences (295). Yet, it is precisely this transgression of boundaries and its consequences that provides Saleem and Guibert both the imperative urge to tell their stories as well as the material with which to tell them.

In order to tell his own life story, Saleem (like Guibert) tells other stories: the history of India's independence and partition, the story of a fantastic community of similarly deviant, gifted children (the Midnight Children's Conference) born, like Saleem, at the hour of independence. To complicate matters, Saleem is not really Saleem; that is, he is not the son of his parents as he (and we) had been led to believe, since he was switched at birth with another child by a nurse in the hospital (117). Therefore, he is the subject and yet not the subject of his own life story; he tells the life story of an Other. In doing so, he races physical disintegration (he believes that he is literally falling into roughly 630 million pieces–the population of India at the time) in an effort to finish the telling of an admittedly distorted and imperfect story of "his" life. Touching on the novel's liminality, David Smale observes that the text functions "in that space between sureties, outside fixed allegiances" (Smale 34).

With Saleem, we see a counterpart to Guibert's liminal revolving-door conversion or poetics of perversion. After an extended failure to join the rest of his family in their "conversion" to new people in Pakistan, the "land of the pure" (309, 310), the perverse Saleem is at last "converted" into a new man after being hit in the head with a spittoon. His amnesia, like conversion, involves a kind of death and rebirth. As a consequence of this "conversion," Saleem becomes other to himself. He becomes the third-person "not-Saleem" in his own narrative, and, as is characteristic of the process of conversion, is given a new name–*buddha*–Urdu for "old man"(350, 360). In that amnesiac suspension of the old self, he is enlisted as a soldier and lost in the jungle in the East Wing of Pakistan (now Bangladesh) during the war of 1971. In this other space–the liminal space of the "dream forest" that is far removed from the "real world"–the buddha and his companions "surrendered themselves"(363). While Rushdie insists that this is the Urdu word *buddha* rather than *the* Buddha, the highlighting of the surrender of self in the dream forest only serves to reinforce the presence of that other Buddha along with the Buddhist principles of *anatman* or "no-self" and the embracing of the true, formless self through a relinquishing of ego. Amnesiac not-Saleem remains in this threshold state until he is bitten by a snake and reclaims his other self in an uncontrolled, hallucinatory flow of narrative in which the story of his life begins to pour through his lips (364-5). When he finally emerges from the forest and passes back over the national frontier between Bangladesh and India, he is symbolically reborn. True to the poetics of perversion, Saleem, like Guibert, transgresses and erodes the boundary that separates the "old" from the "new" self, implying that the latter is always bound to the former or that the self always contains its own other. The conversion-like processes of erasing and reinscribing the self, as they stand in the novel, are more palimpsest than *tabula rasa,* since the erasure of the old and the inscription of the new is never perfect or final. Playfully, yet with deliberately subversive effect, Rushdie manipulates this old/new binary into a paradox. By naming Saleem's new self (the identity of the amnesiac Not-Saleem) *buddha*, or old man, he inverts the traditional terminology of conversion and the converted self inherited from Augustine.

Such perverse, liminal moments of self-narrative, whether characterized by
Berdiaev and Minc as neomedieval crisis or by Hutcheon as opportunities for
challenging, rethinking, de-naturalizing, or de-totalizing (Hutcheon 1989: 62),
are central to this diachronic study and to my articulation of a new middle age.
Rushdie's *Midnight's Children* presents a conflicting view of the crisis of the
self. On the one hand, Saleem insists that the process of self-representation is
a "process of revision" that should be "constant and endless"; it is a process
of which he is obviously proud, if not "satisfied" (460). In this regard, the de-
totalization of the self and its narrative portrayal can be inferred as constructive
if not unproblematically positive. On the other hand, that same process
produces great anxiety and is represented through a series of crises, wherein
the autofictional "I" refers to himself as a "broken creature spilling pieces of
itself into the street" (463). Guibert is a similarly broken creature, and yet, like
Saleem, he also derives a certain authorial "pride" from his special alienation.
Both autobiographers simultaneously lament over and exult in their perverse
liminality and in those things that set them apart from the norm and from
others. Each of them focuses attention on those eccentric differences as both
debilitating and empowering, while leaving the tension between those two
alternatives unresolved.

While the links between Guibert and Rushdie are significant, they are not
unique in their ability mutually to inform their narrative representations of
self as well as to develop a body of evidence in support of the "new middle
age" argument. One could substitute Peter Abelard's *Historia calamitatum*
(1133) for Guibert's *De vita sua* and Eugenides' *Middlesex* (2003) for Rushdie's
Midnight's Children, for example, without altering the terms of that argument.
These and other texts, whether from the original Middle Ages or the so-called
new Middle Ages, present a collective portrait of the self on the margins of
modernity and humanism, that is, a pre-humanist and post-humanist self, a
pre-modern and post-modern (or post-post-modern) self. The terminology is
awkward, and there is no clear sense of whether the present corresponds to
Minc's vision of a post-humanist apocalypse at the end of modernity or to the
kind of fecund opportunity for rethinking modern subjectivity and for self-
reinvention that postmodern, postcolonial, feminist, and other contemporary
theories have posited. The answer is likely a hybrid, to be found in a "grey
zone" somewhere between the two. What is clear is that the present is as much
a "society in transformation" as the twelfth century was in Western Europe
(Morris 37), and just as liminal a moment in terms of the ongoing development
of self. Thus, the present is as much a middle or threshold age as the post-
classical, pre-modern Middle Ages were: a period of transition in which the
self appears equally inchoate.

RYERSON UNIVERSITY

NOTES

1 Hereafter referred to as *De vita sua*. Translated by Benton as "Memoirs."

2 The dates used here are those proposed by John F. Benton who argues against the traditional date of birth of 1053 proposed by Dom Jean Mabillon in his *Annales Ordinis S. Benedicti* (229).

3 I use Linda Hutcheon's definition of postmodern parody here: "repetition with critical or ironic difference" (*Parody* 37). This usage of the term "parody" is in some ways divergent from the more common understanding of parody as satire.

4 My argument, in this regard, is unlike those found in the collection of essays entitled *The New Medievalism*, edited by Marina S. Brownlee et al That work presents innovations in medieval studies, and the application of contemporary theory to medieval works. As such, it does not cover the same diachronic ground that I propose here.

5 The notion that the twelfth century witnessed anything like a renaissance is traced back to 1840. In that year, French scholar Jean-Jacques Ampère proposed that in addition to the "great renaissance of the fifteenth and sixteenth centuries," there had been two other renaissances: one concurrent with the reign of Charlemagne in the ninth century, and another that began around the end of the eleventh century (see Ferruolo 114).

6 Here, Bertens reiterates a similar argument made by Zygmunt Bauman in the Introduction to *Intimations of Postmodernity*. Bauman contends, "All in all, postmodernity can be seen as restoring to the world what modernity, presumptuously, had taken away; as a re-enchantment of the world that modernity had tried hard to dis-enchant" (x).

7 Ian Wood, for example, writes that missionaries "wrote works both of hagiography and of autobiography" (264). He gives Patrick's *Confessio* (fifth century) as one example. Yet he almost immediately concedes that what these texts had were "autobiographical elements" transmitted through "the filters of *topoi*" (265).

8 It is a given that in any autobiographical narrative (not just here in Guibert's), there will be a necessary vacillation back and forth over the frontier of past and present.

9 Rushdie establishes an explicit link between the physical and the textual corpus (*Midnight's Children* 100).

WORKS CITED

Barthes, Roland. *Roland Barthes par Roland Barthes*. Écrivains de toujours. Paris: Seuil, 1975.

Bauman, Zygmunt. *Intimations of Postmodernity*. London: Routledge, 1992.

Benton, John F. *Self and Society in Medieval France: The Memoirs of Abbot Guibert de Nogent*. Medieval Academy Reprints for Teaching. 15. 1970. Toronto: U of Toronto P, 1984.

Berdiaev, Nicolas. *Le nouveau Moyen Âge*. Trans. Jean-Claude Marcadé and Sylviane Siger. 1924. Lausanne: L'Age d'Homme, 1986. Trans. of *Novoe srednevekov'e. Razmyshleniia o sud'be Rossii i Evropy*. (*The New Middle Ages. Reflections on the Destiny of Russia and Europe*). 1924.

Bertens, Hans. *The Idea of the Postmodern: A History*. London: Routledge, 1995.

Bloch, R. Howard. "The Once and Future Middle Ages." *A Journal of Literary History* 54.1 (1993): 67-76.

Brownlee, Marina S. et al., eds. *The New Medievalism*. Baltimore: Johns Hopkins UP, 1991.

Eco, Umberto. *Travels in Hyperreality*. Trans. William Weaver. London and New York: Harcourt, 1986.

Epstein, Mikhail. "On the Place of Postmodernism in Postmodernity." *Russian Postmodernism: New Perspectives on Post-Soviet Culture*. New York, Oxford: Berghahn Books, 1999. 456-68.

Ferruolo, Stephen C. "The Twelfth-Century Renaissance." *Renaissance Before the Renaissance: Cultural Revivals of Late Antiquity and the Middle Ages*. Ed. Warren Treadgold. Stanford: Stanford UP, 1984. 114-43.

Foucault, Michel. "What Is Enlightenment?" *The Foucault Reader*. Ed. Paul Rabinow. New York: Pantheon, 1984.

Freccero, John. *Dante: The Poetics of Conversion*. Ed. Rachel Jacoff. Cambridge: Harvard UP, 1986.

Guibert de Nogent. *Autobiographie: texte et traduction*. Ed. and trans. Edmond-René Labande. Les Classiques de l'Histoire de France au Moyen Age 34. Paris: Société d'Edition "Les Belles Lettres," 1981.

_____. *Memoirs. Self and Society in Medieval France: The Memoirs of Abbot Guibert de Nogent*. Ed. and trans. John F. Benton. Medieval Academy Reprints for Teaching. 15. 1970. Toronto: U of Toronto P, 1984. 34-228.

Hutcheon, Linda. *A Poetics of Postmodernism: History, Theory, Fiction*. London: Routledge, 1988.

_____. *The Politics of the Postmodern*. London: Routledge, 1989.

_____. *A Theory of Parody: The Teaching of Twentieth-Century Art Forms*. London: Routledge, 1985.

Lejeune, Philippe. *Le pacte autobiographique*. Paris: Seuil, 1975.

Minc, Alain. *Le nouveau Moyen Âge*. Paris: Gallimard, 1993.

Morris, Colin. *The Discovery of the Individual: 1050-1200*. Medieval Academy Reprints for Teaching. 19. 1972. Toronto: U of Toronto P, 1987.

Ricoeur, Paul. *Oneself as Another*. Trans. Kathleen Blamey. Chicago: U of Chicago P, 1992.

Rushdie, Salman. *East, West*. 1994. Toronto: Vintage Canada, 1996.

_____. *Midnight's Children*. 1981. Toronto: Vintage Canada, 1997.

Smale, David, ed. *Salman Rushdie:* Midnight's Children/The Satanic Verses: *A Reader's Guide to Essential Criticism*. Toronto: Penguin, 2001.

Stock, Brian. *The Implications of Literacy: Written Language and Models of Interpretation in the Eleventh and Twelfth Centuries*. Princeton, N.J.: Princeton UP, 1983.

Syed, Mujeebuddin. "Midnight's Children and Its Indian Con-Texts." *The Journal of Commonwealth Literature* 29.2 (1994): 95-108.

Weintraub, Karl Joachim. *The Value of the Individual: Self and Circumstance in Autobiography*. Chicago: U of Chicago P, 1978.

Wetherbee, Winthrop. *Platonism and Poetry in the Twelfth Century: The Literary Influence of the School of Chartres*. Princeton, NJ: Princeton UP, 1972.

Wood, Ian. *The Missionary Life: Saints and the Evangelisation of Europe 400-1050*. Harlow: Pearson Education, 2001.

Unmasking the Leper King:
The Spectral Jew in *The Kingdom of Heaven*

Christine M. Neufeld

> The Jew becomes the feminine exalted to the point of mastery, the
> impaired master, the ambivalent, the border where the exact limits
> between same and other, subject and object, and even beyond these,
> between inside and outside, and disappearing – hence an Object of
> fear and fascination. *Abjection itself.* He is abject: dirty, rotten. And
> I who identify with him, who desire to share with him a brotherly,
> mortal embrace in which I lose my own limits, I find myself reduced
> to the same abjection, a fecalized, feminized, passivated rot... (Julia
> Kristeva, "Ours to Jew or die" 185).

Sir Ridley Scott's film *The Kingdom of Heaven* gained some attention both
from the public and academics for addressing what a *Village Voice* film critic
terms "the sociopolitical slag pit" of the contemporary crises in the Middle
East through its imagining of the fragile peace enjoyed by the Latin Kingdom
of Jerusalem in the late twelfth century. Produced as even those Americans in
favor of Bush's global policies had been disabused of the fictions justifying the
American invasion of Iraq, Scott's film offered its audiences a secular revisionist
history of medieval Jerusalem as a multicultural utopia in which the only real
villains are thieving hypocrites and fanatics who preach violence in the name
of religion. A survey of the popular critical reception of the film reveals that
audiences mainly perceived the film's message to be a criticism of religious
fanaticism of all stripes and, despite its carefully crafted carnage, a reflection
on the futility of war. The politics of the film have nevertheless come under
some scrutiny by scholars. However, while Jonathan Riley-Smith and Khaled
Abou el-Fadl (as cited in Sharon Waxman) have argued about which historical
inaccuracies led to the most grievous cultural misrepresentations of Christian
Europeans or Muslim Arabs, the absence of Jews, the third major group with a
history and contemporary vested interest in the Middle East, has gone virtually
unnoted by the film's critics.

This absence should be all the more glaring since the story is set in
what one critic describes as "the usual thousand-year tease," the Holy City of
Jerusalem (Christopher). It seems impossible for audiences not to reflect on
the current Palestinian/Israeli conflict when, at the end of the film's climactic
battle, where we have watched poignantly rendered mass slaughter, the hero
Balian of Ibelin asks Saladin, "What is Jerusalem worth?" and Saladin answers,
"Nothing...Everything."[1] One might conclude that, along with its purported
call for ecumenical tolerance, the other message the film communicates to
audiences inclined to read current events onto its medieval scenes is that, in the
words of the *LA Weekly* film critic, "where men and holy lands are concerned,
the more things change, the more things stay the same" (Foundas). Indeed,
the film's final word on the matter comes in the form of a postscript: "Nearly

a thousand years later, peace in the Kingdom of Heaven remains elusive."
This postscript, however, does not prevent a geographical slippage in the
film's popular reception as an account of ongoing violence between Western
Christians and Arab Muslims. Perhaps, in a world in which an American invasion
of Iraq could be justified in part as a strike against a Saudi terrorist and his
organization in Afghanistan, one should not be surprised to find a filmmaker
treating Jerusalem as Iraq. In a recognizably orientalist move, *Kingdom of
Heaven* presents Jerusalem as a microcosmic Middle East, a move that obscures
the city's unique vexed history as a locus of desire that complicates a simplistic
East/West binary. Framed as an interpretive dilemma: given the film's interest
in at least a semblance of historical realism and its allegorical ambitions, why
are there no Jews in Jerusalem?

Granted, in the late twelfth century the Jews were not a major social
force in Jerusalem. Christian rulers had expelled the Jewish families who had
somehow survived the wholesale massacre that accompanied the Frankish
conquest and occupation of Jerusalem during the First Crusade. In this sense
it is appropriate to have the most direct reference to medieval Jews in the film
be in a description of the hero Balian's own landholdings outside of Jerusalem,
where Christians, Muslims and Jews apparently live and work together. Yet,
historians claim that about forty years prior to Saladin's conquest of Jerusalem
in 1187, and more specifically in the reign of the Leper King Baldwin IV, Jews
were once more visible in the area. Joshua Prawer, the foremost historian of
Jews in the Latin Kingdom, indicates that Jewish communities had succeeded
in reestablishing themselves in most major cities of the kingdom during the
period between 1077 and 1187 (63). Although Jerusalem was the exception,
there is in fact evidence of a Jewish presence in a variety of ways even in the
capital. Adrian Boas goes so far as to suggest that, despite the injunction against
non-Christians returning to the crusader-occupied city:

> some Muslims, along with Jews, returned to the city during the twelfth
> century; they are also recorded on occasion as merchants, pilgrims,
> or expert craftsmen, and perhaps as inmates of the hospital of St.
> John (39).

Bernard Hamilton points out that while few Jews were allowed to live in
Jerusalem, they were allowed to visit and pray at the Western Wall (52, 58).
One such Jewish traveler, Benjamin of Tudela, also confirms that there were
Jewish dyers living in Jerusalem near the Tower of David in 1170 (Boas 40).
Given the film's explicit portrayal of both Baldwin IV and Saladin as idealized
emblems of tolerance, it seems curious not to exploit such historical details to
reinforce the film's vision of Jerusalem as a potential "kingdom of conscience"
that can accommodate all three cultures generated from the Abrahamic religions.
Nevertheless, multiple viewings of the film lead me to conclude there is only
one possible visual representation of a Jew in the entire film, and certainly
no speaking roles. This brief glimpse of the third community with a vested
interest in the occupation of Jerusalem comes, appropriately enough, in the
palace complex in Jerusalem, when the camera pans over a crowd of petitioners

awaiting an audience with Tiberius, the Marshal. Among this variously-costumed crowd appears a bearded man whose robes and head-covering differ from the film's standard depiction of Saracen clothing, perhaps alluding to the garb of the Jewish priestly class through the use of a headdress reminiscent of the *tallit*, a Jewish prayer shawl.

The anachronistic absence of the Jew in *Kingdom of Heaven* becomes most significant when considered in relation to the anachronistic presence of another character in the movie, King Baldwin IV of Jerusalem, known as the Leper King. The historical Baldwin IV was born in 1161 to Agnes of Courtenay and Count Amalric of Jaffa, who later became King of Jerusalem. According to the account of Baldwin's tutor, the historian Archbishop William of Tyre, William himself discovered the first symptoms of what would later be diagnosed as leprosy when the young prince came to live with him at age nine. With Baldwin's symptoms not yet conclusive and medical officials hesitant to misdiagnosis him, the young boy had not yet been identified as a leper when his father died suddenly in 1174. So Baldwin, at thirteen years of age, was crowned the sixth Latin King of Jerusalem. When Baldwin hit puberty the diagnosis of leprosy became unavoidable. According to William of Tyre:

> [He] was seen to be suffering to a dangerous degree from leprosy. It grew more serious each day, specially injuring his hands and feet and his face, so that his subjects were distressed whenever they looked at him (trans. Hamilton 100-01).

Yet no attempt was made to segregate him at any point in his life. Moreover, despite the fact that the illness enervated him and deprived him of the use of one hand, the young king insisted on leading his armies in person and taking part in the fighting until he became too weak to ride. Indeed, in 1177 the sixteen year-old Baldwin led the Franks to a momentous victory over Saladin and his forces at Mount Gisard. Baldwin remained an active head of state, even though by 1183 he was suffering the most devastating effects of his disease. William of Tyre reports:

> [The] leprosy which had afflicted him since the beginning of his reign...became much worse than usual. He had lost his sight and the extremities of his body became completely diseased and damaged, so that he was unable to use his hands and feet. Yet although some people suggested to him that he abdicate and lead a retired life...he refused to surrender either the royal office or the government of the kingdom, for although his body was weak and powerless, yet he was strong in spirit, and made a superhuman effort to disguise his illness and shoulder the burdens of kingship (Hamilton 187).

In the end, Baldwin IV succumbed to complications from leprosy, dying of a fever in 1185, two years before the events of the movie take place. As Hamilton observes: "Few rulers have remained executive heads of state when handicapped by such severe physical disabilities or sacrificed themselves more totally to the needs of their people" (Hamilton 210).

One can hardly blame Ridley Scott and the scriptwriter William Monahan for moving the death of this extraordinary historical figure up a few years. The heroic and apparently tolerant Christian king neatly complements the film's portrayal of the restrained warrior Saladin. A number of film critics comment on what a compelling figure the unbilled Ed Norton cuts as the Leper King, although no one elaborates on the specific nature of his appeal.[2] Doubtless much of the effect is due to the extraordinary costuming that has the king garbed in pure white flowing garments, his facial disfiguration covered by a number of elaborate silver masks. The contrapunctal effect of gauzy fabric and metal mask emphasizes the paradoxical impression of a bodiless voice, an intellect uttering from a metal casing. Nevertheless, the mask teasingly reminds us of what we cannot see, but also cannot forget: the leprous flesh belonging to the bleary eyes peering out from behind the mask. It is this paradoxical portrayal of the King of Jerusalem that should give the attentive medievalist pause to consider how the Leper King functions metonymically for the absent Jew in *Kingdom of Heaven*.

From an historical perspective there is considerable discursive overlap between anti-Semitic discourse and traditional depictions of lepers. A brief consideration of the actual historical attitudes towards lepers and Jews can throw into relief an ideological legacy still operational in the film's popular cultural take on medieval history. On the most general level, stereotypes of Jews and lepers have both functioned historically to construct what Anthony Smith calls "pariah minorities":

> A "pariah minority" is an ethnic or racial group that shares a language and a culture. Its members are the objects of persecution and are viewed by the dominant population as less than fully human—as dirty, inferior, or impure (715).

Scholars such as Jeffrey Richards and Ephraim Shoham-Steiner have observed how both the conceptualizations and treatments of medieval lepers and Jews share a variety of characteristics. The treatment is more than a coincidence of prosecutorial techniques wielded against minorities in medieval Christendom. Sheldon Watts argues that the Fourth Lateran Council's decree in 1215 that both Jews and lepers wear distinctive clothing is a meaningful pairing of the two groups (55). As early as the first century C.E. Josephus, the Jewish historian, recounts a 300-year-old anti-Judaic myth that Jews were driven out of Egypt because they were lepers. "The myth that Jews were particularly prone to leprosy seems to have been among the detritus of learning inherited (via Josephus) from Ptolemaic Egypt" (56).[3] The virulence of this association is evident in a poem by the thirteenth-century Anglo-Norman poet, Walter of Wimborne. The Franciscan's poem, "De Symonia et Avaritia," portrays avarice as an infection issuing from the dying Judas to infect the Jewish people:

> Quondam cum periit Judas suspendio,
> Judeam polluit uentris profluuio;
> nunc fimi fedior fetet effusio
> quam sentit quilibet in morbo regio (115).

In his editorial notes to the poem, A.G. Rigg specifically identifies the infection evoked by the concept of the King's Evil, *morbo regio*, as leprosy. David Nirenberg elaborates the ideological confluence the poem portrays:

> The poem opens with the paradigmatic avaricious act, the betrayal of Jesus by Judas in exchange for a bag of coins. But when Judas hanged himself, his guts poured forth their excrement and polluted the land of Judea (and hence the Jews). His feces...were a *virus*, a slimy, stinking liquid poison, that infected first the homeland (*patria*) and then the Church (*ecclesia*) with avarice. This corruption, this stench could be comprehended only in juxtaposition to the proverbially putrid odor of the leper....From Judas had sprung the avarice most evident among Christians in its dermatological manifestation as leprosy (Nirenberg, 62-3).

Thus, in some instances the construct of leprosy manifests not merely an anxiety about moral contamination, but also a specific association with offences ascribed to the Jews, in particular with relation to the vice of avarice and the trope of the Jew as archetypal traitor.

Though occurring a century and a half after the events we are considering, the Shepherds' Crusade (1320) and the Great Leper Hunt (1321) confirm that this attitude also functioned as a part of medieval crusading ideology. In Watts' opinion: "The horrendous events of 1321 can perhaps be understood as the end product of a conjunction of abstractions: the leprosy construct, the construct of Jews as outsiders, the crusader ideal, and the looming Islamic threat" (62). In the wake of mob attacks on Jews during the Shepherds' Crusade came the rumour of a plot between Jews, Muslims and lepers aimed at the heart of France. According to chroniclers, people believed that the Muslim king of Granada was plotting with the Jews to take over Paris (and by extension the French kingdom) by getting lepers to infect their local wells. In exchange for delivering Paris into the hands of the Muslims through their deployment of French lepers the Jews were to receive Jerusalem and the Holy Land (Nirenberg 65-6). The consequences of this paranoid fantasy fashioning lepers and Jews as co-conspirators were tragic for both communities: lynchings and public executions of lepers and Jews, the destruction of leprosaria in 1321, and the expulsion of the Jews from France in 1323.

As both Nirenberg and Watts independently attest, these persecutions of Jews and lepers were both considered medicinal acts, purging the realm of pollutants that compromised the health of the Christian social body, a purification that continually blurred the boundaries between the literal and metaphorical. Moreover, there is another inherent factor in this prosecutorial phenomenon that conflates these clinical and symbolic paradigms. The concept of the "King's Evil" in Walter of Wimborne's poem reminds us of the tradition of the "royal touch" that attributed to French royalty the ability to heal skin diseases. Consequently, the persecution of Jews had special import for the authority of the king himself. Nirenberg concludes:

It is not surprising, then, that the attack on lepers in 1321 was followed
by an attack on the Jews, especially when we recollect that a king's
ability to heal was believed to be proportional to the zeal with which
he persecuted Jews (63).

While the "royal touch" began in the reign of the second Capetian king, Robert
the Pious (970-1031)—a king whose abilities explicitly included the capacity to
heal lepers [Nirenberg 58]—this alignment of a royal power with literal and symbolic
purification evokes a more ancient legend actually situated in the Holy Land.
In the Apocryphal New Testament, the story commonly called "The Avenging
of the Savior" presents an ancient precedent linking leprosy and Jews to issues
concerning rulership and the occupation of the Holy Land. The story features
encounters between Christians and various diseased Roman rulers who, once
cured, express their gratitude by persecuting the Jews. First Titus, whose face is
disfigured by cancer, hears from Nathan about the death of Jesus of Nazareth,
whose miraculous powers might have cured him. Titus exclaims:

> Woe to thee, O Emperor Tiberius, full of ulcers, and enveloped in
> leprosy, because such a scandal has been committed in thy kingdom;
> because thou hast made such laws in Judæa, in the land of the birth
> of our Lord Jesus Christ, and they have seized the King, and put to
> death the Ruler of the peoples; and they have not made him come to
> us to cure thee of thy leprosy, and cleanse me of mine infirmity; on
> which account, if they had been before my face, with my own hands
> I should have slain the carcases [sic] of those Jews, and hung them
> up on the cruel tree, because they have destroyed my Lord, and mine
> eyes have not been worthy to see his face ("Avenging" 473).

Titus' proclamation of his devotion restores not only his health, but also that
of his extended community: "And when he had thus spoken, immediately the
wound fell from the face of Titus, and his flesh and face were restored to health.
And all the sick who were in the same place were made whole in that hour"
(473). Titus responds to this miracle by acting out the vengeance he vowed
earlier, in effect cleansing the land as he has cleansed the local people: "With
this design, then, they...proceeded to Jerusalem, and surrounded the kingdom of
the Jews, and began to send them to destruction" (473). The legend's climactic
encounter with Emperor Tiberius Cæsar—whose body, the text claims, is riddled
with "nine kinds of leprosy" (472)—reiterates and amplifies the association
of poor government with a diseased ruler, as well as the notion that a ruler's
righteousness can miraculously heal his people:

> Then Tiberius...called him, saying: Velosianus, how hast thou come,
> and what hast thou seen in the region of Judæa of Christ the Lord
> and his disciples? Tell me, I beseech thee, that he is going to cure me
> of mine infirmity, that I may be at once cleansed from that leprosy
> which I have over my body, and I give up my whole kingdom into
> thy power and his.
> And Velosianus said: My lord emperor, I found thy servants Titus and
> Vespasian in Judæa fearing the Lord, and they were cleansed from all

their ulcers and sufferings....And it pleased God Almighty that they went into Judæa and Jerusalem, and seized thy subjects, and put them under that sentence, as it were, in the same manner as they did when thy subjects seized Jesus and bound him....

And [Tiberius] immediately adored the image of the Lord with a pure heart, and his flesh was cleansed as the flesh of a little child. And all the blind, the lepers, the lame, the dumb, the deaf, and those possessed by various diseases, who were there present, were healed, and cured, and cleansed (475-6).

This motif of physically and spiritually cleansed Christians enacting divine vengeance on the Jews through the purification of Jerusalem also functions as a common trope of crusading discourse. Sylvia Schein notes the imagery of pollution and purification that permeates the advocacy of the First Crusade by Baldric of Dol, Robert the Monk, Guibert of Nogent, and Albert of Aachen (15). Consequently, with the Jewish past of the Holy Land looming large in the crusaders' minds, the polemic of conquest characterized the fall of Jerusalem to the crusaders as "yet another punishment meted out to the Jews," the penalty for the Jews' failure to recognize Jesus of Nazareth as the Messiah that justified the Christian occupation of Jerusalem as the new Chosen People (Schein 42). Ironically, this ideology also comes into play in European attempts to grasp the loss of Jerusalem during the historical period depicted in *Kingdom of Heaven*. Writers constructed the fall of Jerusalem to Saladin as "an injury to Christ and to Christendom, and as an act of pollution" (Schein 172). Furthermore, they also suggested that the city's fall was a penalty against the Christians of Outremer, and the particular fault of the inhabitants of Jerusalem. As the *Libellus de expugnatione Terre Sancte per Saladinum* exclaims: "Those Christians were like the evil merchants who sold Christ and the Holy City, and thus they resembled Judas" (qtd in Schein 172). It is this moment of profound ambivalence, of Western self-recrimination and self-doubt—when the Christian confronts the possibility of having become "the Jew"—that the filmmakers choose as the context for their revisionist narrative.

While the makers of *Kingdom of Heaven* would not have access to the complex discursive nexus historically linking leprosy, Jews and crusading ideology outlined above, this history intensifies the theoretical associations that are identifiable in the film. There are three theoretical ways in which a contemporary audience might register a subcurrent aligning the leper and Jew. First, even popular depictions of European history present both lepers and Jews as what I term "intimate strangers." Historically, leper colonies and neighbourhoods that we would now identify as Jewish ghettos both function in the everyday world and yet are not of that world. They are the negative spaces that delimit the parameters of normalcy for medieval European subjectivity. In a similar vein, both the leper and the Jew present European society with the threat of relation. The socially outcast leper was once a member of one's community; similarly, medieval Christianity struggled in various ways with its Judaic roots (Abulafia, Frassetto, Hobbs). The stock image of the Jew as a poisoner in the medieval and early modern periods illustrates how Jews represented an anxiety over contamination, rather than the clear military threat presented by the Saracen outsider.

The notion of contamination leads to the second point: in the Middle Ages both Jews and lepers were associated with what Julia Kristeva would define as "the abject." Kristeva's concept of abjection attributes the fascination and revulsion we feel in the face of refuse and bodily waste to a psychological process:

> The corpse (or cadaver: *cadere*, to fall), that which has irremediably come a cropper, is cesspool, and death; it upsets even more violently the one who confronts it as fragile and fallacious chance. A wound with blood and pus, or the sickly, acrid smell of sweat, of decay, does not *signify* death. In the presence of signified death—a flat encephalograph, for instance—I would understand, react, or accept. No, as in true theater, without makeup or masks, refuse and corpses *show me* what I permanently thrust aside in order to live. These body fluids, this defilement, this shit are what life withstands, hardly and with difficulty, on the part of death. There, I am at the border of my condition as a living being (Kristeva 3).

The repugnance we feel contemplating the decaying, living corpse that is Baldwin IV succumbing to the lepromatous strain of leprosy all too easily demonstrates the anxieties produced when breaches of our bodies' boundaries remind us viscerally of the fragile margins separating us from being lifeless objects. Bettina Bildhauer concisely sums up what "abjection" as a concept has to do with socially marginal groups: "[w]hat violates social categories and boundaries is vilified and excluded; so are bodily excretions" (76). As groups peripheral to the normative social body, both Jews and lepers posed a threat to identity that the medieval imagination somaticized as actual physical pollution.

The association of Jews and lepers with abjection cannot be safely consigned to some "barbaric" medieval past. In his study of the relationships between disease, power and imperialism, Watts observes that colonial physicians perceived leprosy as a condition stemming from racial and cultural miscegenation, rather than as a disease that distinguished the civilized European from the savage. According to Edward Muir of the Calcutta School of Tropical Medicine, leprosy was a kind of "barometer of civilization":

> [Where] we get contact between the primitive and more advanced, there, at the point of contact we find leprosy…unfortunately the more easily adopted features of civilization are often the less credible and are apt to be physically and morally dangerous when not countered by [civilization's] less easily acquired safeguards (qtd. in Watt 81).

The anxiety that Dr. Ross of the Robben Island asylum had, that leprosy was more common among "cross-breeds" of natives and Boers (Watts 81), finds its most sinister echo in Hitler's efforts to "purify" the German *Volk*. Thus, although no longer framed as ritual murderers or bearers of the plague,

Jews also remain haunted by the spectre of the corpse; only this time it is as archetypal victims. I would argue that in the popular imagination Jews are first and foremost identified with the Holocaust. The persistent circulation of images of concentration camp survivors and mass graves continues to foster an ideological association between the Jew and the abject body, both as the potential contaminant of Nazi propaganda and as corpse, the human detritus of Europe's bloody self-fashioning.

One need only consider the gendered dynamics in media depictions of cadaverous concentration camp survivors being rescued by valiant Allied soldiers to recognize another aspect of Kristeva's delineation of abjection: the association of the abject body with the discourse of femininity. The feminization of Jews and lepers provides our entry point into *Kingdom of Heaven*. In the Middle Ages assumptions about the sexual depravity and excesses of both lepers and Jewish men linked both groups to the voracious sexuality deemed the biological characteristic of women since Aristotle.[4] In fact, anti-Judaic folklore in the Middle Ages even purported that Jewish men menstruated (Bildhauer 91). As one of the substances that confounds the distinctions of inside/outside, menstrual blood draws attention to the potential symbolic function of the female body in terms of abjection. In her examination of passages in Leviticus leading up to its prohibitions about leprosy, Kristeva muses: "The shift taking place between chapters 12 and 13 seems significant to me; it goes from within the maternal body (childbirth, menses) to the decaying body [read: leprosy]" (101). Whereas Kristeva explores the alignment of femininity and the Jew with abjection in authors such as Joyce and Céline, for our purposes this association draws attention to the possible symbolic resonances of Baldwin IV in *Kingdom of Heaven*. Recognizing the leper as a feminized figure in the film forces us to confront leprosy's symbolic function in the film as a figure of abjection that gestures toward another "impaired master," the absent Jew.

In contrast to William of Tyre's portrait of a vigorous, if afflicted, young man, the film's conception of Baldwin IV casts him as passive and domesticated. First and foremost, we must reconsider his costuming. Baldwin's mask presents beautiful but androgynous features, particularly when crowned with a headdress looking more like a woman's wimple than a man's headgear. Second, in a narrative that identifies heroism with military feats, Baldwin's enclosure and immobility qualifies his masculinity. We encounter Baldwin first of all in his private chamber, a domestic setting directly in contrast to the political and public scene presided over by Tiberius, the Marshal, immediately preceding it. This domesticity emerges again in Baldwin's final scenes, when he is on his deathbed, and when he lies in state. We do see Baldwin on horseback for his parley with Saladin; but even here we are profoundly aware of his fragility. In fact, the scene serves primarily to display Saladin's integrity in offering to send his physicians to help his obviously suffering opponent. Since the film sets Baldwin up as a surrogate father for the recently orphaned Balian, his physical enervation dramatically juxtaposes him to Balian's biological father,

Godfrey of Ibelin, who at one point boasts of fighting three days with an arrow through his testicle.

In contrast to the film's traditional depiction of medieval chivalry through Godfrey and his companions early on in the film, the character most associated with riding is Baldwin's sister Sibylla. In fact, the filmmakers seem intent on creating a strong association between the two siblings. Of all the film's characters, Baldwin and Sibylla are by far the most orientalized, in that their costuming detaches them from any distinct ethnic or socio-religious identity, removing them from time and history itself. Historians who have considered the unique multiethnic culture of the Frankish Levant indicate that the Franks insisted on distinguishing themselves from their Arab, Byzantine and Jewish neighbours. According to Jacoby:

> The cultural orientation of the Latins settled in the Frankish Levant was shaped by their strong bonds with the West and by their determination to maintain their collective social identity. The members of the Latin nobility expressed their affinity with the nobility in the West in social behavior, rituals, attitudes, mentality, the French they spoke, as well as the courtly literature and legal treatises they read and composed in that language (116).

These distinctions were maintained in sumptuary laws, as well. While the Franks might have used some local textiles, their clothes maintained the distinctive characteristics of Western vestimentary fashions; the Council of Nablus (1120 C.E.) even issued regulations explicitly forbidding Muslims to dress like Franks (Jacoby 107). In the film, however, Sibylla's initial entrances, inevitably accompanied by a flourish of Middle Eastern music, present a princess straight out of the *Arabian Nights*. She is wrapped in diaphanous veils, with jewels dripping off her turban, seductive kohl-rimmed eyes, and hennaed hands. Moreover, she speaks Arabic as comfortably as she does the language of the newly arrived Franks.[5] Her association with her equally exotic brother deepens through a conversation the audience witnesses when she attends his deathbed. Sibylla says to her brother, "You were a beautiful boy. You've always been beautiful. In every way." To which Baldwin responds, "My beautiful sister."

The film carries this idea of Baldwin and Sibylla as reflections of each other to a disturbing conclusion during its climax. Alone in her palace amidst the mayhem of the besieged city, Sibylla shears her beautiful tresses. As she gazes into the marbled mirror before her she momentarily sees in place of her face the ravaged leprous visage of her brother. It is a curious moment, made more so if we recollect that Sibylla is able to see her brother's face in hers only because she betrayed her brother's dying wish. He asked that she remember him as the beautiful boy he once was. Yet when he lies in state she removes his mask to see the disfigured face it hides—a moment created, no doubt, to gratify the audience's own morbid curiosity. The film's visual superimposition of Baldwin on Sibylla to suggest that she imagines herself as a leper is puzzling. For the film shifts here from its sympathetic clinical portrayal of leprosy as Hansen's disease to deploy a traditional construct of leprosy as the somaticization of moral guilt. The vision is the culminating moment in a series of silent shots of a stricken Sibylla absorbing the shock of the siege, watching Balian lead the city while she remains isolated and seemingly insignificant. While accounts of the fall of Jerusalem tell us of Christians shaving their hair as a penitential gesture in the face of an event they perceived as divine punishment, in the film only Sibylla appears thus shorn.[6] One might even see shame in her demeanour, as she hides her face from a passing Balian in the makeshift hospital where she tends the wounded. This portrayal of Sibylla as penitent is confirmed by the film's most ahistorical moment, when Balian demands Sibylla abandon her remaining Latin Kingdom after Jerusalem's surrender, proposing: "Decide not to be a queen and I will come to you." The mute woman Balian finds walking out of Jerusalem with the other refugees, even though, as he observes, "A queen never walks," is a far cry from the woman who accosts Balian before the battle for Jerusalem, exclaiming, "Who are you to refuse a king? I am what I am. I offer you that...and the world."

What remains unclear is precisely what Sibylla is atoning for. Both generic and narrative contexts mitigate the moral ambivalence an audience might feel about the adulterous liaison between Balian and Sybilla. Romance conventions set the tender consummation of their attraction against her obvious distaste for her cardboard villain of a husband, Guy de Lusignan. Moreover, the affair is explicitly legitimated by the permissive context of an orientalized Middle East in which, according to Sibylla, between a man and a woman, "there is only light." Sibylla's plan to have Balian replace Guy as her husband and heir to the Kingdom of Jerusalem is shared by her unequivocally virtuous brother; although they both ultimately recognize that Balian's integrity is too high a price to pay to secure the succession and, by extension, the Kingdom itself. Consequently, if Sybilla as an individual character is not obviously problematic, the audience must contemplate if her curious end suggests that she shoulders the burden of a more general guilt.

The nature of this guilt lies in the film's ambivalent use of the construct of leprosy itself. Given the close identification between the noble siblings, the symbolic use of leprosy to portray Sybilla's ambiguous guilt retroactively modifies Baldwin's significance as the Leper King. Historically Baldwin's reign did create some controversy: Pope Alexander III, in fact, challenged Baldwin's kingship, warning that Jerusalem would fall to its Muslim enemies because a king who was a leper was clearly immoral and out of divine favour (Watts 53). However, until this point the film never portrays Baldwin's leprosy as ideologically problematic. Instead, in Baldwin's first scene, the notion that leprosy is a sinful condition with implications for the Frankish occupation of the Holy Land is dismissed as Saracen mercilessness and superstition, one of the movie's overtly racist moments. Baldwin observes: "The Saracens say that this disease is God's vengeance against the vanity of our kingdom. As wretched as I am, these Arabs believe that the chastisement that awaits me in hell is far more severe and lasting." Ironically, scholarship comparing medieval Christian and Muslim attitudes towards leprosy demonstrates that Islamic theology and

Arabic medical practice presented a more tolerant view of leprosy. Whereas Christian authors drew on Levitical interpretations in the Judeo-Christian scriptures constructing leprosy as divine punishment, the Qu'ran and other Islamic texts generally insisted that the "the blind, the lame and the sick bear no fault or blame (*haraj*), and it is permissible for all men to gather and eat together" (Dols 194).[7] In contrast to the stigmatization of lepers in Christian society, according to Watts:

> Between the seventh and eleventh centuries, medically informed Muslim authors drew on other late antique writers [who treated leprosy as a disease of the body with no moral implications] to present more or less clinically correct descriptions of Hansen's disease....This held that *judhäm, bahq* or *baras* (Arabic words for various forms of clinical leprosy) was one of the hazards of life to be endured; it was not seen as a moral category or as a punishment sent from on high (46).

Consequently, there are no governmental regulations regarding lepers, no rituals of separation or sumptuary laws, or records of communal persecutions in medieval Islamic society (Dols 194). One might even consider the possibility that, given William of Tyre's concern that "our Eastern princes...scorn the medicines of our Latin physicians and believe only in the Jews, Samaritans, Syrians and Saracens" (Prawer 107-08), Baldwin's own extraordinary status as a Christian Leper King had something to do with the unique cross-cultural context in which he lived.

In addition to projecting Christian superstition onto the Muslim Other, the film deploys the positive symbolic valences that could adhere to leprosy in Christian discourse as well. Hamilton argues that Christian opinion on leprosy was in fact divided in the twelfth century, unable to reconcile the Old Testament, priestly interpretations of leprosy as divine punishment with Isaiah's description of the "Suffering Servant" that typologically identified the image of the leper with Christ's Passion (241).[8] The Order of the Knights of St Lazarus, a quasi-monastic order in the Frankish Levant that cared for lepers and which eventually constituted a military order of lepers, illustrates that the latter vision of leprosy played a role in the larger discourse of Christian humility and charity. Indeed, when Baldwin declares, "I am Jerusalem," to Reynald of Chatillon, he becomes the Suffering Servant in contrast to the maniacal warmonger. As he proffers his exposed, ulcerated hand to be kissed by the humiliated Reynald, his leprosy represents a reality the bigot must face about the condition of the Kingdom and the King he serves—a moment that brings to mind the service of lepers by devout medieval Christians, most famously St Francis of Assisi, as a form of *imitatio Christi*. The film explicitly invites its audience to relate Baldwin IV to Christ when the Hospitaler guiding Balian into Jerusalem states that, whereas the Pope commands that Christians kill Arabs, neither Christ nor this king would issue such a command. Throughout the film, then, we see Baldwin IV as the idealized emblem of Christian humility, the Suffering Servant whose virtue distinguishes him from the avarice and violence of the hypocritical ecclesiastical representatives that surround him.

What do we make, then, of this final discomfiting image of Baldwin as the deformed manifestation of Sibylla's self-recrimination? Sibylla's symbolic inheritance of her brother's leprosy and consequent exile sets up the royal family as an aporia reminiscent of the functions of both lepers and Jews in Christian discourse. Watts explains: "Though a leper could be seen as a representative of Christ offering opportunities for Christian charity, the leper was also seen as a sin-curst being who, following the precepts of Leviticus, must be cast out of the community of the faithful" (520). Similarly, Christians from Augustine onwards had struggled with appropriate attitudes towards Jews who on the one hand represented a perfidy that must be annihilated, and on the other an ancestral community that must be tolerated as, to use the famous words of Bernard of Clairvaux, the "living witnesses of our redemption." I would argue the film similarly uses Baldwin to construct its moral centre and simultaneously repudiates him (through his sister) as the obstacle impeding the realization of these very moral ideals. This aporia constructs the Leper King as the spectral Jew. Such a notion finds an actual historical precedent in the fact that shortly after the First Crusade the kings of Jerusalem were symbolically identified with the biblical kings of Judea. Schein observes that Latin rulers called their realm the "kingdom of David," occasionally even going so far as to crown themselves in Bethlehem, rather than Jerusalem, because it was the birthplace of the house of David (96):

> Descriptions of Jerusalem composed in the crusader kingdom expressed the same identification of the Franks with the biblical Israel. ...The crusader rulers of the city were the New Israelites, the new Maccabees, the true successors of Solomon, those who battled the Amalekites and the Edomites (Schein 97).

Just as medieval crusaders acknowledged the legitimacy of Jerusalem as the historical city of the Children of Israel even as they disinherited Jews to fulfill its triumphal Christian destiny, in the film the "kingdom of conscience" that the Leper King seeks to build can only be manifested by Balian's abandonment of its concrete incarnation, Jerusalem. The kingdom built and guided by conscience that Balian's father, Godfrey, tells him to fight for at the beginning of the movie is reduced in the end to a kingdom that exists solely, as Balian tells Sibylla, in one's mind and heart. Moreover, the final gesture that characterizes this kingdom of conscience is a refusal to engage the Other, a choice commendable in terms of crusading militarism, but inadequate as a response to the contemporary "Kingdom of Heaven" that the film's postscript explicitly invokes.

Even as the orientalized portrayal of Sibylla should give one pause, more disturbing is her final transformation. Balian's demand of the penitent and progressively more westernized-looking Sibylla that she give up her queenship—not to mention lands much more powerful than Jerusalem—in order to begin an anonymous life with him in France, ultimately bespeaks a discomfort with the breakdown of boundaries between Self and Other that the film otherwise wants to endorse. In Kristeva's words:

> It is thus not lack of cleanliness or health that causes abjection but what disturbs identity, system, order. What does not respect borders,

positions, rules. The in-between, the ambiguous, the composite. The
traitor, the liar, the criminal with a good conscience.... (4)

To cast Sibylla in the end as a leper suggests her identification as a traitor, a
powerful trope of anti-Semitic discourse, and one that draws attention to her
most distinguishing characteristic: her culturally ambiguous nature. The film
depicts the Latin Kingdom's royal family as orientalized Europeans with feet in
both the East and the West. They are the inheritors of a Jerusalem gained at the
cost of bloodshed, a community whose European origins do not entirely cancel
out their intimacy with the Saracen Other, both as opponent and neighbour.
The royal family of the Latin Kingdom of Jerusalem, whose familiarity masks a
difference and vice versa, must be extricated from the Holy Land and assimilated
in order for the Franks and Saracens to find a comfortable resolution in the
neat categories of aggressor and victim, occupier and occupied.

The specific tragedy of Jerusalem and its environs, whose populations
suffer from political and social dynamics far more tangled than the occupation of
Iraq, emerges most distinctly in the final moments of *Kingdom of Heaven*. What
do we make of Jerusalem, the principle, the homeland, the prison, the haven,
the war zone? Balian's war-speech, better than anything, illustrates how any
political allegory of Western crusading in the East is confounded by Jerusalem's
history: "None of us took this city from Muslims," he declares. "We fight over an
offence we did not give." Such a claim, as Michael Atkinson points out in his
review, could easily issue from the lips of a second generation Israeli. "What is
Jerusalem?" our hero continues, "Your holy places lie over the Jewish temple
that the Romans pulled down. The Muslim places lie over yours." "Which is
more holy," Balian inquires, "the Wall, the Mosque, the Sepulchre?" "Who has
claim? No one has claim; all have claim." "We defend this city, not to protect
these stones, but the people within these walls," he concludes. The cross-shots
to Sibylla listening sombrely to his speech suggest this is a lesson she, too, needs
to learn. Like her brother, her identity has been bound to the city of Jerusalem.
From a medieval perspective she, like the Jews of old, is guilty of literalism, of
mistaking the material for the spiritual. The film's pronouncements on Jerusalem
consistently construct it as paradox: a site that is everything and nothing, to
which all and none have claim. This Jerusalem is utopian in the Greek sense: it
is "not a place." Thus, even as the film proffers a vision of a tolerant multiethnic
society, the narrative conveys its impossibility; for tolerance appears in the end
as homogenization and segregation, reinforcing the binaries the film ostensibly
dismisses. The burden placed on Sibylla's and Baldwin's shoulders is to bear
the guilt of those who do not know or have their place, those who threaten the
limits of the Western self. What the film cannot confront in them is the proximity
between Self and Other that places needs at painful cross-purposes, a proximity
whose unexpected affinities might also hold the potential for radical change and
the possibility of alliances rather than merely uneasy truce.

EASTERN MICHIGAN UNIVERSITY

NOTES

1 All quotations from the movie are based on my own transcription of the dialogue.

2 James Sanford, for example, refers to Ed Norton's performance as "memorable" in his review.

3 In his assessment of leprosy in terms of imperialism, Watts asserts that because Christians drew on Old Testament sources for their understanding of leprosy, leprosy was thought of in terms of Jews. For example, "a learned French medical advisor to Emperor Ménélik II of Ethiopia, one Father Mérab, stated around 1920 that 'to understand the rules governing this quintessentially biblical disease once common among Jews, it is enough to read Chapter XIII of Leviticus'" (Watts 74).

4 See Richards 106-7 and 160. See also Watt 56.

5 Jacoby claims that "with few exceptions, Frankish familiarity with Arabic remained limited to daily usage" (107).

6 For an account of this see Schein 159.

7 As this citation implies and Dols later explicitly states, Muslim medical practitioners did not believe that leprosy was terribly contagious — a fact confirmed by current medical research (see Watts). These practices still pertain in later times. Watts observes that Christian missionaries were troubled that Muslims did not place lepers in a special moral category (82).

8 The Levitical treatment of leprosy can be seen in Numbers 12: 1-5; 2 Kings 5: 21-72; 2 Kings 15: 1-5. The "Suffering Servant" passage that for medieval thinkers prefigured Christ's Passion is Isaiah 53: 3-4.

WORKS CITED

Abulafia, Anna Sapir. "Christians and Jews in the High Middle Ages: Christian Views of Jews," *The Jews of Europe in the Middle Ages (Tenth to Fifteenth Centuries): Proceedings of the International Symposium Held at Speyer, 20-25 October 2002.* Ed. C. Cluse. Turnhout, Belgium: Brepols, 2005. 19-28.

Atkinson, Michael. "Holy Crap: The Empire Strikes Back." *The Village Voice* May 3, 2005. http://www.villagevoice.com/film/0518,atkinson1,63635,20.html. Accessed 14 March 2008.

"The Avenging of the Saviour" *The Ante-Nicene Fathers: Translations of The Writings of the Fathers down to A.D. 325* Ed. Cleveland Coxe. 10 vols. Edinburgh, 1860s; New York: Christian Literary Company, 1885; repr. Grand Rapids: Erdmans, 1978. 8: 472-476.

Bildhauer, Bettina. "Blood, Jews and Monsters in Medieval Culture" *The Monstrous Middle Ages.* Eds Bettina Bildhauer and Robert Mills. Toronto and Buffalo: University of Toronto Press, 2003. 75-96.

Boas, Adrian J. *Jerusalem in the Time of the Crusades: Society, landscape and art in the Holy City under Frankish rule.* New York: Routledge, 2001.

Christopher, James. "*Kingdom of Heaven*" *The Times* 5 May 2005. http://entertainment. timesonline.co.uk/tol/arts_and_entertainment/film/article388257.ece. Accessed 14 March 2008.

Dols, Michael W. "The Leper in Medieval Islamic Society," *Speculum* 58.4 (1983): 891-916.

Foundas, Scott. "O Jerusalem: Ridley Scott goes medieval on us." *LA Weekly*, May 5, 2005. http://www.laweekly.com/film+tv/film/o-jerusalem/667/. Accessed 14 March 2008.

Frassetto, Michael. "Heretics and Jews in the Writings of Ademar of Chabannes and the Origins of Medieval Anti-Semitism." *Church History* 71.1 (2002): 1-15.

Hamilton, Bernard. *The Leper King and his Heirs: Baldwin IV and the Crusader Kingdom of Jerusalem*. Cambridge: Cambridge UP, 2000.

Hobbs, Kathleen. "Blood and Rosaries: Virginity, Violence and Desire in Chaucer's 'Prioress's Tale,'" *Constructions of Widowhood and Virginity*. Eds Cindy Carlson and Angela Weisl. New York: St. Martin's Press, 1999. 181-98.

Jacoby, David. "Society, Culture and the Arts in Crusader Acre" *France and the Holy Land: Frankish Culture at the End of the Crusades*. Eds Daniel H. Weiss and Lisa Mahoney. Baltimore and London: The Johns Hopkins University Press, 2004. 97-137.

The Kingdom of Heaven. DVD. Dir. Ridley Scott. 2005; Beverly Hills, CA: Twentieth Century Fox Home Entertainment, 2005.

Kristeva, Julia. *The Powers of Horror: An Essay on Abjection*. New York: Columbia UP, 1982.

Nirenberg, David. *Communities of Violence: Persecution of Minorities in the Middle Ages*. Princeton: Princeton UP, 1996.

Prawer, Joshua. *The History of the Jews in the Latin Kingdom of Jerusalem*. New York: Oxford UP, 1988.

Richards, Jeffrey. *Sex, Dissidence and Damnation: Minority Groups in the Middle Ages*. London and New York: Routledge, 1990.

Riley-Smith, Jonathan. "Truth is the First Victim." *The Times* 5 May 2005. http://entertainment.timesonline.co.uk/tol/arts_and_entertainment/film/article388261.ece. Accessed 15 March 15 2008.

Sanford, James. Review. "*Kingdom of Heaven*," May 5, 2005. http://www.interbridge.com/jamessanford/2005/kingdomof.html. Accessed 14 March 2008.

Schein, Sylvia. *Gateway to the Heavenly City: Crusader Jerusalem and the Catholic West (1099-1187)*. Burlington: Ashgate, 2005.

Shoham-Steiner, Ephraim. "An Ultimate Pariah? Jewish Social Attitudes toward Jewish Lepers in Medieval Western Europe." *Social Research* (Spring 2003): 1-22.

Smith, Anthony D. "The Politics of Culture: Ethnicity and Nationalism, *Companion Encyclopedia of Anthropology*. Ed. Tim Ingold. London: Routledge, 1994.

Walter of Wimborne, "De Symonia et Avaritia." *The Poems of Walter of Wimborne* Ed. A.G. Rigg. Toronto: Pontifical Institute for Mediaeval Studies, 1978. 111-143.

Watts, Sheldon. *Epidemics and History: Disease, Power and Imperialism*. New Haven: Yale UP, 1997.

Waxman, Sharon. "Film on Crusade Could Become Hollywood's Next Battleground." *The New York Times*, 14 August 2004. http://query.nytimes.com/gst/fullpage.html?res=9400E3DF163FF931A2575BC0A9629C8B63. Accessed 15 March 2008.

The Sights and Sounds of the Body and Soul in Morris' "The Defence of Guenevere" and "King Arthur's Tomb"

Suzanne J. Clark

At a pivotal moment in James Joyce's novella, "The Dead," the character Gabriel, gazing up at his wife Gretta, "ask[s] himself what is a woman standing on the stairs in the shadow, listening to distant music, a symbol of." Here, Gretta is motionless—appearing almost as a statue that invites a gaze—and is figured "as if" she were a "symbol of something" (370). Gretta's silence renders her auditorily missing, just as the shadow over her, generated by a blockage of light, cloaks her form and colour and renders her all but absent. Gabriel's desire to know his wife through symbolic means lies at the heart of the work's interest in knowing that which is absent, not least "the dead" of the work's title, by turning to the senses. The yearning to classify and, by extension, to understand the represented figure of the female based on symbols extends back in Western culture at least as far as the literature and legends of the Middle Ages and is at play in various renditions of the Arthurian tale of Launcelot and Guenevere written since the fourteenth century. Yet, these re-workings of the legend have all too rarely centred their narrative on the question: what is it that women want? Rather than asking what a woman represents, how, with a voice, might she represent herself?

In the first Pre-Raphaelite volume of poetry, William Morris contends with prior representations of the figure of Guenevere by presenting her side of the story of her relationship with Launcelot and by giving her a voice, and, by extension, agency. This paper will consider Morris' unique contribution to the school of Arthurian writings[1] and demonstrate how he recovers female agency in the legend of Guenevere and Launcelot in his Arthurian poems "The Defence of Guenevere" and "King Arthur's Tomb" by turning attention to the senses.

The primary source for Morris' Arthurian poems was Robert Southey's edition of Sir Thomas Malory's *Le Morte d'Arthur*, which he and Edward Burne-Jones read together in 1855. Morris remained intrigued by the work and in 1857 he reportedly read the fifteenth-century saga aloud to Burne-Jones and Rossetti as they painted in Rossetti's studio (Mancoff 331). Throughout the Victorian and Edwardian periods, *Le Morte d'Arthur* was regarded as "a book for gentlemen" and "a reference book for the 'modern knight'" (Bryden 74)—and not without good reason. Malory "present[s] a social structure and a gentlemanly ideal recognizable to the Victorians, who attached great importance to the notion of class" and "the strong patterns of male friendship and to the brotherhood of knights bound by oath"(Bryden 74). However, what was largely missing from the Arthurian romance was a dynamic representation of the female perspective, which Morris consequently placed at the centre of his work.

The majority of critics has suggested that Morris differed from his contemporaries (Carlyle and Tennyson, for instance) in that his medievalism did not view the ideals of the Middle Ages as being the ideals of Victorian culture and he refused to present men of the Middle Ages in the guise of Victorians in fancy dress. Rather, Morris valued the Middle Ages "as the antithesis of modern values"(Riede 1992:67). To Morris and the Pre-Raphaelite poets and painters generally, the "return" to the medieval was not an idealized return to the Middle Ages with Victorian Christian virtues in tow. Instead, their use of the past as "aesthetic" was, as David Riede notes, not a "backward-looking art," but a modern art that challenged assumptions about "the relation of art to conventional morality and to society at large...reveal[ing] not the cohesion of medieval society, but the fragmentation of modern society"[68]. Moreover, whereas before Morris it was fashionable to "frolic with the medieval past," with him "it became a matter of faith to revive the past"(Agrawal 247), and the works of the revival offered a stage for the Pre-Raphaelites to interpret and represent serious social matters. The Pre-Raphaelite circle defied conventional morality, privileged beauty over duty, and turned to the medieval as a "sensually liberated and liberating antidote to Victorian prudery, earnestness, and high seriousness"(Riede 55). More than just a release, Pre-Raphaelite works of art and poetry set in the Middle Ages explored historical realism and the efficacy of historical revivalism, ultimately affecting the reinvention of Arthur and the presentation of Queen Guenevere.

Three years before the appearance of *The Defence of Guenevere*, Owen Meredith (first earl of Lytton) published a collection of Arthurian poems entitled *Clytemnestra, The Earl's Return, The Artist, and Other Poems*. Inga Bryden maintains that "[b]oth Meredith's and Morris' poems are characterized by intensity of detail and colour, yet distinctively they both explore the protagonists' psychological tensions"(100). Furthermore, she finds parallels in the relation between the "voyeuristic objectification of the female form and the portrayal of the characters' inner states or subjectivities" in Morris' and Meredith's Arthurian works. Bryden's observations are especially valuable because they serve to highlight the importance that Morris and Meredith placed on physical and visual representations of their female characters. One difference between the poets is that in the title poem of Morris' volume, Guenevere seems to be instructing her accusers, transforming them into voyeurs, which enables her to reclaim her body through this assertive act of directing others' gazes. Guenevere peppers her monologue with verbs in the imperative as she commands and makes direct requests of her listeners, most often demanding that they be attentive to their senses: "*Listen*, suppose your time were come to die" (16); "There, *see* you, where the soft still light yet lingers...?" (124); "*say* no rash word /against me, being so beautiful" (223-24); "*See* my breast rise" (226); "*See* through my long throat" (230); and "*look* you up, / And wonder..." (234-35) ("The Defence of Guenevere," emphases mine). Particularly with respect to the directives surrounding her corporality, Guenevere makes use of her body and takes ownership of it, in order to present it to the onlookers in exchange for time until Launcelot's arrival. Moreover, the numerous questions that she poses to her accusers supplement her imperative commands, for they also serve the same function of delay. In posing questions, she makes demands of her accusers, prompting them to pause and consider what she has asked them. For instance, when she skilfully inquires, "will you dare, / When you have looked a little on my brow, / To say this thing is vile?" (236-38), the engaged spectators (and readers), in order to arrive at an answer, must shift their thoughts away from Guenevere and toward their own conceptions and (visual) perceptions of her. For once, no longer a Philomela-figure, Guenevere can straightforwardly direct her accusers and their sensory perceptivity.

The figure of Guenevere is presented in Meredith's Arthurian poetry as highly eroticized and beautiful, which makes her "the focus of the poem... although she does not utter a word"(Bryden 101). Her speechlessness is what most prominently distinguishes her from the Guenevere offered by Morris. In the period of their composition, Morris' Arthurian poems were most commonly considered in opposition to the series of Arthurian poems by Alfred Lord Tennyson, which would later constitute his *Idylls of the King* (1856-1885). Not unlike the Pre-Raphaelite poets, Tennyson's creative contribution to the Arthurian canon of literature came from adding a psychological aspect to the legends through recounted vision and dream sequences. Yet, this innovation resulted in an inner world that was able to privilege the cognitive in many ways, but largely ignored the body. Those readers sympathetic to Morris' poems might find Tennyson's too focused on the transcendental, structured through recounted vision and dream rather than through physical and physiological experience. Furthermore, Algernon Charles Swinburne felt that in excising the morally tainted elements of the Arthurian legend, "Mr. Tennyson ha[d] blemished the whole story"(39). Tennyson's Arthurian heroine, like Meredith's and Malory's, is not an agent, but rather an object to be seen and discussed. What makes Morris' Guenevere so original is that she is presented as a communicator and not as "a means of communication" (Bryden 99). Morris' Guenevere is impressive in her rhetorical strategy and oral delivery, making her an active participant rather than the passive figure capable only of producing the reactive emotions found in prior depictions of her.

For Maurice Merleau-Ponty, the body is "a system of perceptual powers" and as such, gaze, touch, and all other senses are together "powers of one and the same body integrated into one and the same action"(1999:166-67). For a true and accurate perception—or in this case, experience—of a thing, multiple senses are needed. Moreover, the object of perception presented to one of the senses exercises a form of agency, calling upon the "concordant operation of all others"(166). Just as an orchestral piece of music without colour may be said insufficiently to capture its audience, the story of Launcelot and Guenevere requires a synesthetic experience of integration and unification rather than mere articulation of the senses in order to give the legend new life.

Morris' title poem, relying so heavily on verbal performance, foregrounds speech as Guenevere's most powerful means of defence[2] and "her most potent weapon in testing God's attitude toward her as she searches for and tentatively discovers divine approval of her actions with Launcelot"in "King Arthur's

Tomb" (Post 319). In both poems, performance and speech merge and draw attention not only to what is reportedly spoken, but also to how it is articulated. Readers are asked to be attentive to the lovers' speech in the same way they might examine an orator's delivery, where the written text becomes secondary to verbal transmission and its accompanying nonverbal communication. In this way, Guenevere's speech becomes a sensory experience for the reader, just as it would presumably have been for the accusers or witnesses within the poem. As Hartley Spatt puts it, "Morris' early works attempt to transform the raw data of history and legend into formal memories of characters and scenes"(4). Because words offer records of the memories of a moment, the dialogue afforded to Guenevere and Launcelot opens possibilities for readers to look into the characters in a way that a mere recounting of their actions does not permit. The more the story appears introspective, the more readers are compelled to feel rather than simply process what is being recounted.

Linked with speech, audition also plays an important role in both poems. In "The Defence of Guenevere," the ability to hear, integral to any form of dialogue between characters, is what ultimately alerts Guenevere to her knight's arrival and the forthcoming rescue:

She would not speak another word, but stood
Turn'd sideways; listening, like a man who hears
    His brother's trumpet sounding through the wood
    Of his foes' lances. She lean'd eagerly,
And gave a slight spring sometimes, as she could
At last hear something really...(287-92)

When the queen ceases to speak, all attention is turned toward the incoming Launcelot. Similarly, "King Arthur's Tomb" concludes with a moment of auditory perception when Launcelot awakens and says:

"I stretch'd my hands towards her and fell down,
    How long I lay in swoon I cannot tell:
My head and hands were bleeding from the stone,
    When I rose up, also I heard a bell." (393-6)

Albertus Magnus claims that "something is not secure enough by hearing, but it is made firm by seeing," and he quotes Horace's assertion that "things intrusted to the ear / Impress our minds less vividly than what is exposed / To our trustworthy eyes"(qtd. in Carruthers 17). This connection between audition and vision is an important one for Morris' Arthurian poems, not least because it underscores the need for Guenevere to persuade her accusers with more than dialogue, making the experience of her defence a multisensory one.

In her study of the politics of sight and the optical determinants in *The Defence of Guenevere and Other Poems*, Lindsay Smith contends:

Guenevere's method is to present her defence in the form of optical arguments, including the condition of a transparent body, and the causes of colour. Indeed, her absolute reliance upon the agency of the eye, upon her faithful documentation of visual phenomena, operates in the text as an example of the inevitability of complexity and paradox in all acts of interpretation. The difficulty of linguistic defence is articulated principally through occasions of visual perplexity or trickery of the eye; an optical debate is selected as best dramatizing the complexities and paradoxes of linguistic defence (188).

For Morris, the sensory experience of vision lies at the heart of "The Defence of Guenevere" and "King Arthur's Tomb." In the former, Guenevere asks her accusers to imagine the visual demands of the choosing cloth parable to illustrate the optical paradox at work within the poem and Guenevere's own rhetorical monologue. She instructs them: "here, see!...and you to ope your eyes...to see / A great God's angel" (25-28), as well as to look on her body: "see...See... look you up" (226-37). More than this, perhaps the strongest evidence for the centrality of vision in the poem comes in the final lines of "The Defence":

> as she could
> At last hear something really; joyfully
> Her cheek grew crimson, as the headlong speed
> Of the roan charger drew all men to see,
> The knight who came was Launcelot at good need (291-5).

In this closing stanza, in keeping with the terza rima scheme, the poem's three-line stanza pattern is altered by the addition of a fourth line that, effectively, ties up the end of the poem with a completed rhyme. Morris uses the form of the terza rima to its highest potential, as we, accustomed to the steady rhythm of the interlocking tercets, expect the stanza to end on the word "see," but instead, the poem ends with a vision—a knight arriving in due time and, as the spondee on the final foot foregrounds the litotes, in "good need."

Moreover, in terms of vision, physical gestures play a key role in the poems' presentation of psychological strife being expressed through the body. At many points, it is the body that reacts before the subject is conscious of the cause. In "King Arthur's Tomb" Launcelot's body responds prior to mental awareness: "And he, being tired too, was scarce aware/Of her presence; yet as he sat and gazed,/A shiver ran throughout him, and his breath/Came slower" (116-19). Similarly, Guenevere's body reacts in a visible way some thirty lines later: "After, a spasm took/Her face, and all her frame...terribly she shook" (146-48). Furthermore, in "The Defence," the narrator prefaces Guenevere's second speech with a salient image of "passionate twisting of her body there" (60) that visually demonstrates her internal conflict.

Consideration of visual perception in Victorian poetry also requires attention to photography and other optical inventions. Lindsay Smith aptly notes:

> Even though the works of Ruskin, along with those of Morris and the Pre-Raphaelites, clearly share a common desire to privilege the eye, critics have nevertheless underestimated the commitment of the two writers to specifics of the workings of visual perception, and to the eye as an organ rendered newly enigmatic by photography and other contemporary optical inventions (12).

The emergence of photography in the first half of the nineteenth century changed the way in which people were seeing the world and also how they thought about the act of seeing itself. Ruskin and Morris were attentive to this shift and, in their texts of the 1840s and 1850s, they shared "a promotion of a new type of sovereignty assigned to the eye"(17). Though poetry might at first seem tangentially related to photography, Susan Sontag, in *On Photography*, claims that "[p]oetry's commitment to concreteness and to the autonomy of the poem's language parallels photography's commitment to pure seeing"(96). The invention of the camera in Europe in the 1830s significantly altered cultural investment in the visual; the camera's presence transformed acts of looking, calling faithful transcription into question.

More than this, the details of photographing a subject brought questions of selection and fragmentation into the mix. Because "nobody takes the same picture of the same thing.... [P]hotographs are...not just a record but an evaluation of the world"(Sontag 88). As in photography, so in poetry that retells a well-known legend, every inclusion and exclusion must be seen as intentional. The poet's established boundaries become like the photographer's picture frame. In his Arthurian poems, Morris captured the same scene as other poets; however, he framed his opening two poems with a strong attention to Guenevere and the details of perception surrounding her. Morris, with his sharp and trained eye and with vivid detail, put into words the scene that he saw in his imaginative replaying of the legend.

In *Camera Lucida*, Roland Barthes suggests that, "[p]hotography has something to do with resurrection"(82) and indeed, by extension, it relates to intentional rewritings of past folklore. When analysing a shot, it becomes important to consider what the photograph captures within its frame, as well as what is excluded or left out of the picture space. Just as with other senses, what is absent can be as important as what is present, particularly since it requires the observer mentally to create that which is missing. Even in the Middle Ages, the link between vision and cognition was well known. In fact, in the medieval period, "seeing and knowing [were] practically inseparable" and the visual experience is what primarily verified and predicated being (Burke 18).

Ruskin states that for the human soul "to see something, and tell what it saw in a plain way" is its greatest achievement; the sense of sight is instrumental to understanding both art and the world (287). Ruskin made it his mission to open the eyes of men "to the richness and delicacy of all that is to be seen around them," since he was ultimately interested in "vindicating the rights of the senses"(Hough 8,12). While some theorists have argued that heightened perceptual awareness is generated through a concordance of the senses, Ruskin accomplishes the same end (attentive perception) through a more focused education of the visual sensibilities. Naturally, given his interest in art and architecture, Ruskin privileges the sense of sight as a means through which routinely neglected objects and details within our visual field are brought to cognizance. In Morris' work, the primacy of the visual is less determined than it is for Ruskin. Graham Hough oscillates between two understandings of the visual in Morris' work when he writes in *The Last Romantics*, "The fact is that Morris is not much interested in art as the mere expression of visual sensibility"(92), and later adds that the "[l]ove of the visible world was always the dominant sentiment in Morris's mind"(129). This variance seems to imply a discord between Morris' experience and expression of the visual. I suggest that Morris highlights the visual experience of Guenevere while also moving beyond a "mere expression of visual sensibility" in order to illuminate (through dialogue) the *invisible* that exists beyond what is seen. Like Joyce's Gabriel, Morris prompts readers to question and interpret what lies beyond the frames of both visual and auditory perception.

The division between the visible and the invisible operates on many levels in Morris' poetry and in nineteenth-century England. The society's provisional solution for dealing with depraved and reprobate issues, such as prostitution, was to cast a shadow over them, while spot-lighting the merits of morality. In many ways, the Pre-Raphaelites were dis-coverers who in their craft sought to re-cover what society had attempted to render invisible. While Rossetti expressed interest in the subject of prostitution—we might think of "Jenny"—his real interest "seem[ed] to lie in the bafflement of a man confronting the problem of female sexuality"(Riede 1992:57). For Morris, the concern for female sexuality extends beyond what is seen into what is heard. In "The Defence of Guenevere" and "King Arthur's Tomb," Morris brings forward a parallel to the visible/invisible division by effectively moderating what is audible in order to uncover what is inaudible. Given that Guenevere is granted speech (in the form of monologue and dialogue) in Morris' poems, it becomes possible for the first time in nineteenth-century recastings of the Arthurian legend to turn attention to what lies beyond her words.

Throughout the first two Arthurian poems in *The Defence of Guenevere and Other Poems*, Guenevere takes her body and soul into her own hands and doubly saves herself, both from her accusers in "The Defence" and from a terrible fate in "the aftertime" (367) in "King Arthur's Tomb". Though Launcelot arrives to rescue her at the end of "The Defence," Guenevere is equally involved in saving Launcelot in "King Arthur's Tomb." Her plea, "Help me to save his soul!" (208), emphasizes both the power and the responsibility that she takes upon herself.

Bryden argues that in Walter Pater's famous review, "Poems by William Morris," he finds that Guenevere's body functions as a textual effect: "'the poem…is a thing tormented and awry with passion, like the body of Guenevere were defending herself from the charge of adultery'"(106). More than a textual effect, what was apparent to some critics (and particularly to Robert Buchanan) was the visual and tactile presence of the sexualized female body in the volume's opening Arthurian poems. In his 1872 essay, "Fleshly School of Poetry and Other Phenomena of the Day," Buchanan, a cardinal critic of the fleshly in the nineteenth century, finds himself unable to assess the value of the poems given this bodily focus. Because of this presence of the body in the poems, he reluctantly incriminates Morris alongside Rossetti and Swinburne—to Buchanan's mind, the chief propagators of what is vile—for having an "ever-present undertone of fleshliness" in his poetry (Buchanan 70). In "The Defence of Guenevere" and "King Arthur's Tomb," Guenevere's body, however sensual, plays as important a role as her actions and dialogue, not least because of its function as a sight and site of beauty.

In the Middle Ages, at the time of Malory's writing of *Le Morte D'Arthur*, beauty was an aesthetics of proportion conceived of as "something intelligible, a kind of mathematical quality" and a quantitative experience (Eco 43). In poetry, the appeal of a particular line was discussed empirically, based on metre and rhythm and judged on the basis of proportion. Bodily beauty was also adjudicated quantitatively, on the same basis. A passage from Gilbert of Hoyt's twelfth-century writings offers a definition of the "correct dimensions of the female breasts, if they are to be truly pleasing." It reads: "The breasts are most pleasing when they are of moderate size and eminence"(qtd. in Eco 11). The medieval clergyman continues his definition, but in doing so, links the aesthetics of the female body with a larger issue of female agency by saying that breasts "should be bound but not flattened, restrained with gentleness but not given too much licence." That the female breasts must be restricted from having too much licence suggests that they present a threat and might have a will of their own. Should they undertake to function as something other than a nurturing or aesthetic object, they could be dangerous. In "The Defence of Guenevere," Arthur's Queen addresses her accusers, instructing them and directing their gaze: "see my breast rise,/Like waves of purple sea, as here I stand" (226-27). At this point in the poem, Guenevere not only emphasizes her physical presence, but also invites an evaluation of her shapely form, "being so beautiful" (224). The image that she likens to her breast, "waves of purple sea," gives readers the visual impression of a palpitating chest rising and falling and exercising a good deal more "licence" than Hoyt's standards would allow. The water imagery of the stanza also causes us to take the verb "stand" at the end of the sentence in its nautical definition of sailing or steering a boat in a specified direction. In this sense, Guenevere becomes a vessel steering and directing the course, which offers a further support for the conception of Morris' Guenevere as a female character with agency. In this image, Guenevere has figuratively taken over the helm, just as her breast has, in flowing as the waves, taken much licence.

As for symbolic representation (so central to many of the Pre-Raphaelite works of art), in the Middle Ages, "it was appropriate that the things of God should be symbolized by very dissimilar entities...because it was precisely the incongruity of a symbol that made it palpable and stimulating"(Eco 55). We see Morris incorporating this interplay in what is perhaps the most psychologically salient instance of symbolic representation in the poems—the parable of the choosing cloths that, as was seen earlier, Guenevere herself stages: "'One of these cloths is heaven, and one is hell,/Now choose one cloth for ever'" (22-3) she says, and further instructs, "you must somehow tell" "which they be" (24, 23). In telling the parable of the choosing cloths, Guenevere is asking her audience of accusers, by analogy, to understand her moral dilemma. "[O]ne...was blue,/...and one...red;/No man could tell the better of the two" (34-

36), she adds. The expected iconography of the cloths seems to have gone terribly awry for the choosing subject of Guenevere's tale, where, even with an appeal to God for help, the selected blue cloth signifies "hell." Guenevere's fable and symbols are captivating and enable the Queen to "make intelligible those doctrines which proved irksome in their more abstract form"(Eco 54). In so doing, Guenevere offers her audience both an experience and a defence, as Morris moves beyond the realm of the symbolic and below the surface, to the realm of sensory experience.

For D.S.R. Welland, a painter gives "what the writer cannot give, with all his advantages, the visible aspect of things"(44). The writer can only suggest the visible image that the painter (or photographer) can offer. I would argue that Morris' attention to and inclusion of the visual produces a similar effect; the body and soul can become one in the same way Welland finds possible in a painter's craft. In the medieval tradition, Guenevere fashions her bodily beauty as "gracious proof" of her goodness, where a lovely exterior substantiates a moral interior. With a privileging of the senses, what is most readily perceptible becomes the standard by which Guenevere would have us judge her. Since it is not possible visually to perceive another's spiritual self, if a strong correlation exists between the invisible state of one's soul and what can be physically seen, heard, or touched, it becomes a much simpler task to interpret the body as accurately representing the soul.

Moreover, Guenevere's ability to speak seems inextricably tied to her physical self, for her effort to verbalize memory is "a literal bodying forth of language"(Bryden 106). In the moments before her second speech in "The Defence," the narrator describes Guenevere:

She stood, and seemed to think, and wrung her hair,
Spoke out at last with no more trace of shame,
With passionate twisting of her body there.... (58-60).

Indeed, as much as her inner soul supposedly manifests itself outwardly in the form of beauty, the road is not unidirectional. That Guenevere can touch and experience herself and is, in fact, compelled to do so suggests both that her outward experience affects her inner state and that touch, the primary way the body interacts with the world, figures as a central field of perception in both poems. "The Defence of Guenevere" opens with the image of touch:

But, knowing now that they would have her speak,
She threw her wet hair backward from her brow,
Her hand close to her mouth touching her cheek,
....yet felt her cheek burned so,....
She must a little touch it...(1-7).

Through this abrupt beginning to the poem we are not given the accusation that has brought about Guenevere's trial, but instead are presented with the physical description of the queen who is chiasmically (recall Merleau-Ponty) "touching her cheek,/As though she had had there a shameful blow" (3-4). At this moment she is both the subject and object of her touch, and seems to be thus experiencing herself experiencing herself, as she would have her observers do. Another prominent instance of touch comes in "King Arthur's Tomb," where Launcelot looks on as Guenevere embraces the tomb, which seems to offer her the strength she needs to renounce him:

> "lo you her thin hand,
> That on the carven stone can not keep still,
> Because she loves me against God's command….(274-76).

By touching the tomb, Guenevere gains power to stop herself from touching Launcelot—"not / Ever again shall we twine arms and lips" (196-97), she proclaims—and instead she prays to Christ, that he might provide her with the strength to keep her "hot lips" from touching too "near his brow" (207).

A common feature of "The Defence of Guenevere" and "Arthur's Tomb" is that both collect and coalesce the senses, rather than exclude or privilege one point of view or one method of experience. In this sense, Morris is doing something with the Arthurian stories that Malory would not have thought to do given that "medieval theories of art are invariably theories of formal composition, not of feeling and expression"(Eco 41). Morris supplements the medieval tale of Launcelot and Guenevere by adding senses and feeling while also adhering to and extending beyond medieval aesthetic principles. In placing Guenevere at the centre of his poems, Morris was contributing to an aesthetic that Rossetti also presented pictorially. In his study of Pre-Raphaelite art and design, Raymond Watkinson maintains that the viewer of a Pre-Raphaelite painting was not asked to

> compare what he saw, framed and hanging on a wall, with other
> objects prescribed as noble works of art, but with his own experience
> of the kind of objects or figures depicted, to assess the relations of
> figures not by their conformity to the rules of art, but the probability
> of human behaviour (175).

It was because the young painters challenged and pushed the eyewitness experience to its limit that they "had such an impact, were so much feared by the academicians, so excitedly pursued by the new patrons"(175). Certainly, the point of view offered in Morris' opening Arthurian poems exhibits this quality more than any other contemporary rewriting of the Arthurian story.

One problem with any return or recasting of earlier literary or cultural material is overcoming the inevitable tension between present and past. According to Riede, the Victorian poet could not be "both wholeheartedly medieval and wholeheartedly modern"(Riede 1984:85). Like that of the other Pre-Raphaelite artists, Morris' medievalism was not a means to treat the religious, moral, or political concerns of the time, but rather a means to aestheticize the prevailing medieval conditions, making it the task of the reader to take meaning from the work and introspectively apply it to modern concerns. In the opening poems of *The Defence of Guenevere and Other Poems*, Morris seems divorced from his age and, in keeping with the Pre-Raphaelite commitment to nature, portrays Guenevere not as a character of plot, but as a self-directed, sensual figure. In doing so, Morris recovers Guenevere's agency in a way earlier poets, with their mute and unembodied Gueneveres, did not.

In *William Morris: Romantic to Revolutionary,* E.P. Thompson suggests that Morris' single greatest intellectual strength was a "powerful historical imagination" that allowed him to reconstruct the Middle Ages "neither as a grotesque nor as a faery world, but as a real community of human beings"(28). According to Thompson, in this reconstructed world "Morris found a place, not to which he could retreat, but in which he could stand and look upon his own age with the eyes of a stranger or visitor, judging his own time by standards other than its own"[28]. William Morris created a fresh approach to translating the Arthurian material where the focus was not on recounting the legends with added moral directives for the times, but rather on recovering the legend and its heroine by making it an experience of the senses for characters and readers alike.

UNIVERSITY OF WESTERN ONTARIO

NOTES

1   Given the number of prevalent and comprehensive studies of the history of the legend itself (see Lacy, for example), I will not attempt to include historical details in this essay, except where such details are pertinent to my argument.

2   Her defence is, as many critics including David Riede have noted, "really no defense at all, but only a declaration that moral choices are difficult and that beauty and passion are irresistibly more attractive than social responsibility" (1984: 100). In titling the poem, and volume, as a "defence," Morris is, like his Arthurian heroine, playing with the limits of the presented case and the accusations brought against her.

WORKS CITED

Agrawal, R.R. *The Medieval Revival and Its Influence on the Romantic Movement.* New Delhi: Abhinav Publications, 1990.

Barthes, Roland. *Camera Lucida.* Trans. Richard Howard. New York: Hill and Wang, 1981.

Bryden, Inga. *Reinventing King Arthur: The Arthurian Legends in Victorian Culture.* Aldershot: Ashgate Publishing, 2005.

Buchanan, Robert. *The Fleshly School of Poetry.* New York: Garland Publishing, 1986.

Burke, James. *Vision, the Gaze, and the Function of the Senses in* Celestina. University Park: Pennsylvania State UP, 2000.

Carruthers, Mary. *The Book of Memory: A Study of Memory in Medieval Culture.* Cambridge: Cambridge UP, 1990.

Eco, Umberto. *Art and Beauty in the Middle Ages.* Trans. Hugh Bredin. New Haven: Yale UP, 2002.

Hough, Graham. *The Last Romantics.* London: Gerald Duckworth, 1949.

Joyce, James. "The Dead." *Dubliners.* Eds. Hans Walter Gabler and Walter Hettche. New York: Garland Publishing, 1993.

Lacy, Norris, ed. *The New Arthurian Encyclopedia.* New York: Garland Publishing, 1996.

Mancoff, Debra. "Morris, William." *The New Arthurian Encyclopedia*. Ed. Norris Lacy. New York: Garland Publishing, 1996. 330-31.

Merleau-Ponty, Maurice. "The Natural World and the Body." *The Body: Classic and Contemporary Readings*. Ed. Donn Welton. Malden: Blackwell, 1999.

_____. *The Visible and the Invisible*. Evanston: Northwestern University Press, 1968.

Morris, William. *The Defence of Guenevere, and Other Poems*. 1858. Ed. Margaret A. Lourie. New York: Garland Publishing, 1981.

Post, Jonathan. "Guenevere's Critical Performance." *Victorian Poetry* 17.4 (1979): 317-27.

Riede, David. *Dante Gabriel Rossetti Revisited*. New York: Twayne, 1992.

_____. "Morris, Modernism, and Romance." *ELH* 51.1 (1984): 85-106.

Ruskin, John. *Modern Painters*. Vol. 3. London: George Routledge, n.d.

Smith, Lindsay. *Victorian Photography, Painting and Art: The Enigma of Visibility in Ruskin, Morris and the Pre-Raphaelites*. Cambridge: Cambridge UP, 1995.

Sontag, Susan. *On Photography*. New York: Picador, 1977.

Spatt, Hartley. "William Morris and the Uses of the Past." *Victorian Poetry* 13.3 (1975): 1-9.

Swinburne, Algernon Charles. *Under the Microscope*. New York: Garland Publishing, 1986.

Thompson, E.P. *William Morris: Romantic and Revolutionary*. London: Merlin Press, 1977.

Watkinson, Raymond. *Pre-Raphaelite Art and Design*. London: Trefoil Publications, 1990.

Welland, D.S.R. *The Pre-Raphaelites in Literature and Art*. Freeport: Books for Libraries Press, 1969.

Dante Gabriel Rossetti's "The Staff and Scrip" and Related Pictures

D.M.R. Bentley

On 18 September 1849, Dante Gabriel Rossetti wrote to his brother William Michael informing him that he had recently purchased, for five shillings, a two-volume translation of the *Gesta Romanorum*, adding: "I was however rather disappointed, having expected to find lots of glorious stories for poems. Four or five good ones there are; one of which...I have considerably altered, and enclose for your opinion" (*Correspondence* 1:93). This was the genesis of "The Staff and Scrip" (then entitled "The Scrip and Staff"), the literary ballad that, according to his brother, Rossetti worked up from a prose draft into a poem between 1851 and 1853 and, on the evidence of the manuscripts in the Humanities Research Center at the University of Texas, revised substantially before its first publication in the *Oxford and Cambridge Magazine* in December 1856.[1] Further revisions of the poem prior to its appearance in *Poems* (1870) and *Poems* (1881) resulted in a piece that has attracted relatively little and quite sharply polarized critical attention. To Graham Hough, it is "overloaded and too merely poetical...without relevance to anything but previous literature" (69) but to Gabriel Sarrazin it contains "l'idée mère de la poésie de Rossetti," "le grand Amour extatique des moines et des chevaliers" (242, 245). Between these extremes (and in accordance with William Michael Rossetti's dating of it to 1851-53), critics have tended to regard "The Staff and Scrip" as a well-achieved but far from complex work whose principal interest lies either in a pictorialism that is typical of Rossetti's poems of the Pre-Raphaelite period (1848-53) or in a medievalism that anticipates the work of William Morris and Edward Burne-Jones.[2] When examined in relation to its sources and in the context of Rossetti's contemporaneous watercolours of medieval subjects such as *Chapel before the Lists* (1856-58) and *The Wedding of Saint George and the Princess Sabra* (1857), the 1856 version of "The Staff and Scrip" emerges as a rich and complex poem in its own right—one in which the dialogues between body and soul and sexual desire and religious faith in the medieval Christianity that it appropriates and evokes collapse towards the fusion and blending that Walter Pater famously captures and celebrates in his observation that, "like Dante, [Rossetti]...knows no region of spirit which shall not be sensuous also, or material" (221).

I

From the number of volumes purchased by Rossetti in September 1849, there can be no doubt that the primary source for "The Staff and Scrip" was the Reverend Charles Swan's two-volume translation of the *Gesta Romanorum*, which was published in London in 1824. As Wynnard Hooper points out in his re-edition of Swan's translation, there are two tales, numbers 25 and 66, in this version of the *Gesta Romanorum* that obviously supplied the "groundwork" (117n) for Rossetti's poem.[3] Swan himself, in a note to tale number 66, refers the reader back to "Tale XXV, which differs but little" (2:231n). In fact, "The Staff and Scrip" appears to be an amalgam of both these tales. In the first, entitled "Of Ingratitude," a "pilgrim" fights a "tyrannical king" on behalf of a "noble lady...on condition that, if he fell in battle, his staff and scrip should be retained in her private chamber, as a memorial of his valour, and of her gratitude" (1:113-14). The protagonist of "The Staff and Scrip" is also a pilgrim who dies fighting for a beleaguered lady, but, unlike her counterpart in the tale, she retains his staff and scrip in her chamber and remains constant to him. In the second tale, entitled "Of Constancy," a "certain Knight" becomes enamoured of a lady of "great beauty" and fights a "tyrannical duke" who has "won her to dishonour." True to the knight's wishes, she hangs "his bloody[4] armour in her hall" and, like the heroine of Rossetti's poem, visits the *memento* of his sacrifice often and elects "to remain single to the end of her life" (2:229-31). Clearly, Rossetti's poem owes a debt to both of these tales and not just to the first, as William Michael and others have erroneously assumed.[5] Indeed, while it derives its title and central figure from the first tale, "The Staff and Scrip" is closer in manner and spirit to the second. Moreover, the very fact that Rossetti drew on one tale concerning a pilgrim and another concerning a knight helps to explain the dual identity of his protagonist as both a "Pilgrim" in search of revelation and a "knight" in the service of a lady (*OCM* 771,773; *CPP* 19, 24) and, as such, an early embodiment of the marriage of sacred and profane love to which he gives glowing pictorial expression in *The Wedding of Saint George and the Princess Sabra.*

Although "The Staff and Scrip" is unmistakably indebted to tales 25 and 66 in Swan's translation of the *Gesta Romanorum*, certain aspects of the poem indicate that its "groundwork" extends considerably further. In the letter with which he enclosed the prose draft of the poem, Rossetti told his brother that he had recently spent "several days at the [British] Museum...reading up all manner of old romaunts, to pitch upon stunning words for poetry" and "deriv[ing] much enjoyment from the things themselves, some of which are tremendously fine" (*Correspondence* 1:93). Perhaps at this time, or when versifying the poem in 1851-53, or, most likely, when revising it for publication in the *Oxford and Cambridge Magazine,* Rossetti appears to have "read up" the one-volume edition of *The Old English Versions of the Gesta Romanorum* that was edited for the Roxburghe Club by Sir Frederick Madden in 1838. The pertinent tale in this edition, "Emperor Fredericus" (number 9), is an alternative version of Swan's "Of Constancy" that is drawn largely from Harleian MS 7333 in the British Library. Several of its words and phrases, such as the knight's request to the "demeselle" to hang his "bloody serke on a porche afore" (23), would doubtless have appealed to Rossetti, but it was in a quotation from one of Madden's notes that he probably found the basis of the stanza in "The Staff and Scrip" in which the heroine opens the pilgrim's scrip hoping to find "letters writ to calm/Her soul" (*OCM* 755; *CPP* 55). The quotation in question—"and in his sherte was wryten this verse, Thynke on hym and haue mynde, that too the was soo Kynde" (506)—is drawn from the version of the *Gesta Romanorum* that was printed by Wynkyn de Worde, a text with which Rossetti was extremely unlikely to have been directly familiar because the only extant copy of it is in the library of St. John's College, Cambridge. Joseph Knight and R.L. Mégroz both adduce *The Old English Versions of the Gesta Romanorum* as the sole source for "The Staff and Scrip," and the former considers the substitution of the pilgrim's staff and scrip for the knight's "bloody serke" "false to the sincerity of [Rossetti's] ordinary workmanship" (65). This is a dubious claim at best, and it becomes more so if Madden's edition was merely a supplementary source for the poem, a likelihood strengthened by the fact that the stanza in which Rossetti's heroine seeks comforting words in the pilgrim's scrip was added, as the manuscript indicates, during the process of revision prior to the poem's publication in the *Oxford and Cambridge Magazine*.[6]

Rossetti need not have looked any further than the "Application[s]" and "Moralité" of the three *exempla* upon which "The Staff and Scrip" draws to discover the parabolic interpretation of their pilgrim and knight. In all three cases, the protagonist of the tales is glossed as Christ, the antagonist as the Devil, and the lady over whose fate they do battle the soul of mankind. The most elaborate of these glosses is the "Moralité" to "King Fredericus," where the seduction of the lady by the tyrant and her subsequent rescue by the knight is likened to the loss of Edenic innocence and the redemption of fallen Man by Christ, who "drowe matrimony with us, that is to say...tooke our kynde, and hayde batail agenst the Deville" (24).

A reader coming to the poem with these and similarly straightforward allegorical expectations will quickly find them complicated, however. In the 1856 text, the poem is preceded by an epigraph—Ophelia's song from *Hamlet* 4.5.23-26—that transforms the Pilgrim into a lover:

"How should I your true love know
    From another one?
By his cockle-hat and staff
    And his sandal-shoon." (*OCM* 771)

Nor do the names given to the heroine and her antagonist in the opening stanza provide allegorical certainty to a reader familiar with St. Luke's legendary devotion to the Virgin Mary, let alone possessed of the specific knowledge that he was a tutelary figure for the Pre-Raphaelites[7] and that white lilies (*blanche lys*) are emblematic of the Virgin's innocence in *Girlhood of Mary Virgin* (1848-49), *Ecce Ancilla Domini!* (1849-50), and other Marian works by Rossetti:

"Who owns these lands?" the Pilgrim said.
    "Stranger, Queen Blanchelys."
"And who has thus harried them?" he said.
    "It was Duke Luke did this:
        God's ban be his!" (*OCM* 771; *CPP* 19).

A straightforward interpretation of Queen Blanchelys[8] is yet further complicated when she is introduced sitting "idle by her loom" and "sicken'd" by the "sweetness" of "musk and myrrh," for the Virgin Mary is typically depicted busily weaving or sewing (as in *Girlhood*), "musk" is redolent of sexuality, and "myrrh" is associated with death as well as the Epiphany.[9]

To the extent that he is not given a name, the Pilgrim who enters this interpretatively complex scenario can be seen as an Everyman figure in the tradition of *The Pilgrim's Progress*, a work to which Rossetti on at least one occasion—in July 1858—referred his own life (*Correspondence* 2:227). Unlike Bunyan's Christian, however, the Pilgrim of "The Staff and Scrip" is not in the midst of a journey with, in Rossetti's words, "the pitfalls plain to the eye & all the wicked people with wicked names" (*Correspondence* 2:227) and, although, like Christian, he is *en route* from this world to that which is to come, he is also in the midst of a more geographically-specific journey back from the Holy Land. This fact, which explains the presence of some "dust of palm" rather than "letters writ to calm/[The Queen's] soul" in his scrip, identifies him as a "Palmer"—that is, by Dante's definition in the *Vita Nuova*, one of the pilgrims "who go beyond the seas eastward, whence often they bring palm-branches" (*Works* 345, and see 346).[10] It also points towards Dante as the shaping force in Rossetti's conception of the Pilgrim in "The Staff and Scrip," an inference supported by his portrayal, first of Dante himself and then of his guiding principle of Love ("Dantis Amor"), as a pilgrim in an 1852 sketch for "Dante at Verona" and in the various versions of *Dante's Dream at the Time of the Death of Beatrice* (1856, 1871, 1880).[11] There seems little, if any, doubt that the love for Beatrice that has its origins in the *Vita Nuova* and its completion in the *Paradiso* lies at the heart of "The Staff and Scrip" and underwrites the ritualistic and momentous exchange of salutations between the Pilgrim and Queen Blanchelys when they first meet:

> The Pilgrim said, "Peace be with you,
>   Lady;" and bent his knees.
>   She answer'd, "Peace." (*OCM* 772; *CPP* 19)

The "light stalls of golden peace" (*OCM* 775)[12] in Heaven that God grants to the Pilgrim and Queen Blanchelys at the end of the poem confirm that their initial exchange and mutual pledge is indeed a Dantean *saluto*—a soteriological greeting and pledge on earth that is repeated and fulfilled in Paradise.[13]

Contributing to this comic pattern is the occurrence of variations of the phrase "here and there," first in the Pilgrim's statement of his belief in God's omniscience that precedes his encounter with Queen Blanchelys, then in the conversation following their salutation, and finally in the first of the three concluding stanzas that describe their heavenly reunification. In the first instance, the Pilgrim is addressing a stranger who has informed him of the Queen's plight; in the second, he is in dialogue with the Queen, and in the third, the speaker is the poem's omniscient narrator:

> "Friend, stay in peace. God keep thy head,
>   And mine, where I will go;
> For He is here and there;" he said.
>   He pass'd the hillside, slow,
>   And stood below.

. . .

She gazed at him. "Your cause is just,
   For I have heard the same:"
He said: "God's strength shall be my trust.
   Fall it to good or grame,
     'Tis in His name."
"Sir, you are thank'd. My cause is dead.
   Why should you toil to break
A grave, and fall therin?" She said.
   He did not pause but spake;
     "For my vow's sake."
"Can such vows be, Sir,—to God's ear,
   Not to God's will?" "My vow
Remains. God heard me there as here,"
   He said with reverent bow,
     "Both then and now."

. . .

Stand up to-day, still arm'd, with her,
   Good Knight, before His brow
Who then as now was here and there,
   Who had in mind thy vow
     Then even as now. (*OCM* 771, 772, 775; *CPP* 19, 20, 24)

Although the precise nature of the Pilgrim's "vow" is not disclosed,[14] the implication is that it, together with his unwavering faith, has assured his salvation (and perhaps that of Queen Blanchelys). This is even clearer in the manuscript, where more is made of the Pilgrim's "vow" and greater emphasis is placed on his "reveren[ce]" through references to his "pray[ing] within himself," "kneel[ing] in prayer" in "empty churches," and seeking absolution from a priest.[15]

Yet, as the description of the Pilgrim's response to the Queen's face and body indicates, his journey to the Holy Land has been spiritually unrewarding and he seems at first blush to be mistaking sexual attraction for spiritual experience:

Her eyes were like the wave within;
   Like water-reeds the poise
Of her soft body, dainty thin;
   And like the water's noise
     Her plaintive voice.
For him, the stream had never well'd
   In desert tracts malign
So sweet; nor had he ever felt
   So faint in the sunshine
     Of Palestine.
Right so, he knew that he saw weep
   Each night throughout some dream
The Queen's own face, confused in sleep

With visages supreme
　　Not known to him. (*OCM* 772; *CPP* 19-20)
No explanation is offered for the Pilgrim's experience of *déja vu* or his sense
of an affinity between Queen Blanchelys and the "visages supreme"[16] that he
probably cannot know until after death, but the gist of these stanzas is clear
enough: the Pilgrim has found a human focal point for his "vow" that accords
with his belief in an omnipresent God and satisfies his hitherto unslaked
spiritual thirst. As even the flowing *enjambement* of the second and third
stanzas indicates, he has gained from Queen Blanchelys an inner peace that
eluded him in the Holy Land and a motivating purpose through which to
fulfill his vow.

　　Nevertheless, his sensual and "confused" response to the Queen raises
doubts about his spiritual state that are not allayed by his behaviour when he
receives the knightly accoutrements that she sends him for his coming battle
with Duke Luke:

She sent him a sharp sword, whose belt
　　About his body there
As sweet as her own arms he felt.
　　He kiss'd its blade, all bare,
　　　Instead of her.
She sent him a green banner wrought
　　With one white lily stem
To bind his lance with when he fought.
　　He writ beneath the same
　　　And kiss'd her name.
She sent him a white shield, whereon
　　She bade that he should trace
His will. He blent fair hues that shone,
　　And in a gold space
　　　He kiss'd her face. (*OCM* 773; *CPP* 20-21)

To the extent that it confirms the Queen's desirability and the Pilgrim-knight's
devotion to her, this eroticized arming scene functions metaphorically, but
it also continues the troubling of interpretive certainty that began with the
poem's opening stanzas. Is the behaviour of the knight a proper display of
dedication through which his chivalric devotion is rightly deflected away from
the Queen's person or is it an improper display of sexual desire indicative of
confusion, misdirection, or a lack of restraint?

　　From the severely anti-fleshly perspective of a Robert Buchanan or a John
Morley, the answer would probably be the latter, and, indeed, a negative
assessment of the Pilgrim-knight's behaviour seems to be sustained by the
description of his accoutrements and Queen Blanchelys' responses after his
body is returned from his victorious but fatal encounter with Duke Luke:

His sword was broken in his hand
　　Where he had kiss'd the blade.
　　　"O soft steel that could not withstand!

> O harder heart unstay'd,
>   That pray'd and pray'd!"
> His bloodied banner cross'd his mouth
>   Where he had kiss'd her name.
> "O East, and West, and North, and South,
>   Fair flew these folds, for shame,
>   To guide Death's aim!"
> The tints were shredded from his shield
>   Where he had kiss'd her face.
> Oh of all gifts that I could yield,
>   Death only keeps its place,
>   My gift and grace!" (*OCM* 774 22-23)

Apparently, the Pilgrim-knight's erotic behaviour has had a corrosive and fatal effect on his sword, banner, and shield, transforming each in its own way into an accomplice of death. In conjunction with what the reader knows of the Pilgrim-knight's behaviour and earlier response to the Queen, her perception of herself as the cause of his destruction, particularly her identification of "Death" as her salient "gift," align her with the *femme fatale*, a figure that would begin to occupy a central position in Rossetti's work in the early 'sixties with *Joseph Accused before Potiphar* (1860). That in *Poems* (1870 and 1881) the "folds" of the Queen's banner become a "web," a word by then associated by Rossetti with the deadly attractions of Lilith (*Poems* 54; *CPP* 23 and 161 ["Body's Beauty"]) suggests that he himself came more to recognize the affinity between Queen Blanchelys and the *femme fatale*.

If "The Staff and Scrip" had ended with the return of the Pilgrim-knight's body, an attribution of blame for his death could plausibly be assigned to his behaviour and, with the addition of a dose of misogyny, to its *provocateuse*. It does not so end, however, and the two remaining portions of the poem—the stanzas that describe the Queen's constancy and the stanzas that describe her reunion with the Pilgrim-knight in Heaven—provide grounds for a very different interpretation. Ronnalie Roper Howard expresses dismay that after the Queen's "highly emotional" response to the sight of the Pilgrim-knight's dead body ("'O pale that was so red!/O God, O God of grace!/Cover his face'" [*OCM* 774; *CPP* 22]) she continues to "bewail...his death" (61), but her ensuing behaviour is surely necessary to indicate the depth of her grief, the extent of her mourning, and the firmness of her faith. After the "damsel" to whom they have been entrusted presents the Queen with the Pilgrim-knight's "staff and scrip" they are "hung above her bed," where they will remain for "Five years, ten years" (*OCM* 774; *CPP* 23). On the night of his death, they shake with "the passion of her grief" and by morning they are "wet with tears." On later occasions, "she would wake with a clear mind/That letters writ to calm/Her soul l[ie] in the scrip" but find only "Pink shells, a torpid balm/And dust of palm" (*OCM* 775).[17] Such is the Queen's faith that she is neither deterred by this lack of assurance nor prevented by inconsolable grief from participating in the dances, hunts, and other "palace sport[s]" that are part of a "Queen's

life" (*OCM* 775; CPP 23). With the work of mourning complete, she is able
to live fully and happily, without, however, forgetting or forsaking the Pilgrim-
knight whose staff and scrip continue to "h[a]ng above her bed" and "above
her head"—that is, to occupy a paramount position in her life both physically
and psychologically.[18]

The final three stanzas of the poem are set off from the preceding narrative
not only by a shift in setting from earth to Heaven, but also by shifts in
tense (to the present) and mood (to the imperative) that align them with the
"Application"s or "Moralité"s that follow the tales in the *Gesta Romanorum*:[19]

> Stand up to-day, still arm'd, with her,
>> Good knight, before His brow
> Who then as now was here and there,
>> Who had in mind thy vow
>>> Then even as now.
> The lists are set in Heaven to-day,
>> The bright pavilions shine;
> Fair hangs thy shield, and none gainsay;
>> The trumpets sound in sign
>>> That she is thine.
> Not tithed with days' and years' decease
>> He pays the wage He owed,
> But in light stalls of golden peace,
>> Here in His own abode,
>>> Thy jealous God. (*OCM* 775; *CPP* 24)

Drawn from God's fierce condemnation of idolatry in Exodus 20:4-5—"Thou
shalt not make unto thee any graven image...for I the Lord thy God am a
jealous God"—the poem's closing words proclaim emphatically that the love
of the God who has reunited the "Good knight" and Queen Blanchelys in
the "Golden peace" of Heaven is one that will "tolerate no unfaithfulness or
defection in the loved object" (*OED*).[20] In addition to confirming that the
Pilgrim-knight's devotion to the Queen was not an act of infidelity to God, the
affirmative concluding vision of "The Staff and Scrip" invites a reconsideration
of the seemingly fatal consequences of his conduct on the eve of his fatal
battle with Duke Luke. In treating the sword, shield, and banner as objects
of erotic desire did he behave idolatrously and incur God's wrath? Is (self-)
destruction the consequence of deflecting sexual desire from its proper goal?
Are sexuality and death, passion and violence, interconnected? Such near-
Freudian extrapolations would seem far-fetched if they did not call to mind
other works of the same period and later by Rossetti, Morris, and, of course,
A.C. Swinburne that raise similar questions in increasingly daring ways—
Rossetti's *Lady Lilith* (1864-68), Morris' "The Wind" (1858),[21] and Swinburne's
"Anactoria" (1866) being but three cases in point. In its treatment of sexuality,
as in its idiosyncratic use of Christian significances, "The Staff and Scrip" is a
transitional poem that recalls Rossetti's work of the Pre-Raphaelite period even
as it anticipates developments to come.

II

In his now under-valued *Survey of English Literature, 1830-1880,* Oliver Elton labels "The Staff and Scrip" "a typical Pre-Raphaelite poem" both in its apparent "simplicity" and "because it falls naturally into four pictures, or panels, representing the meeting [of the Pilgrim and Queen Blanchelys], the arming [of the Pilgrim-knight], the vigil [of the Queen and her ladies], and the return [of the Pilgrim-knight's body]" (2:13).[22] Along similar lines, Florence Boos observes that the "Queen's lament over the dead Pilgrim resembles roughly a Morrisean tableau, although no situations [in Morris's work] are precisely parallel" (131). No "precise...parallel[s]" to the "four pictures" of "The Staff and Scrip" are to be found in Rossetti's work either, but there are certainly correlations of mood and imagery between the poem's arming scene and the scene depicted in *Chapel before the Lists* (1856-64), a small watercolour that was in progress by January 1856—that is, nearly a year before the appearance of the poem in the *Oxford and Cambridge Magazine*.[23] It was at that time that the combination of *Chapel before the Lists* and *Fra Pace*[24] prompted Ford Madox Brown to observe that in painting "the world of our fathers with its 4 chief charackteristicts, Religion, Art, Chivalry & love" Rossetti had found "[h]is forte...[as] a lirical painter & poet & certainly a glorious one" (163).

As its title indicates, the setting of *Chapel before the Lists* is a chapel, where the two central figures, a knight and a lady, are kneeling and embracing. In front of the knight and behind the lady is an altar surmounted by a chalice and lit by two tapers. Hanging from the knight's back is a shield decorated, as in "The Staff and Scrip," with a portrait of the lady "blent [in] fair hues." The lady herself faces what appears to be an open grave, lit by two candles on a cruciform candle-holder and flanked by a long-handled grave-digger's spade. In her right hand she holds the scabbard and in her left the belt of a large cruciform sword with which she appears to be arming the knight. When Brown saw the painting, the opening behind the couple showed "in the distance a 'blacke tower' & beside it a 'blacke' knight mounted, waiting with his lance in rest for the combat" (163). As the painting now stands, however, the distance is occupied by the accoutrements of the lists, and directly behind the knight's head, an ecclesiastical procession. Not only do the circumambient religious objects and setting recall the Pilgrim-knight's faith in an omnipresent God, but the presence of the grave and spade also recalls Queen Blanchelys' conviction that in coming to her aid he is "'toil[ling] to break/A grave, and fall therein'" (*OCM* 772; *CPP* 20). If there is an equivalent to the staff and scrip in the painting, it is the "gryphon" (or griffin) whose "crowned head" and winged torso surmount the knight's helmet at the front and right of the picture space. A composite of the head of an eagle and the body of a lion, the gryphon is described by John Ruskin in *Modern Painters* 3 (1856) as a "profound expression of the most passionate symbolism" and "an acknowledged symbol...of divine power" in whose "unity of lion and eagle, the workman of the middle ages always meant to set forth the unity of the human and divine natures" (3:112).[25] A gryphon appears in the climactic cantos of the *Purgatorio* as a representation of "the union of the divine and human nature in Jesus Christ" (Cary 307n4), first drawing "A car triumphal" (29:103) and then reflected in Beatrice's "beaming eyes" (31:119).[26] That the lady in *Chapel before the Lists* gazes pensively towards the gryphon on the knight's helmet aligns her with Beatrice and, like the confluence of religion and love in the painting as a whole, suggests that the couple's devoutness sanctifies their passionate embrace and promises its continuation beyond the grave. Moreover, since one of the gryphon's traditional roles is as a guardian of young women, the knight's helmet could well serve, like the Pilgrim-knight's staff and scrip in Rossetti's poem, as an aid to memory and a prompt to constancy.

While the reunion of lovers takes place in Heaven in "The Blessed Damozel" (in both the poem and, later, the painting) and, of course, in the concluding stanzas of "The Staff and Scrip," the entirely happy union of lovers on earth is limited in Rossetti's work to a few sonnets in *The House of Life* and to a few paintings of the mid-to-late 'fifties and early 'sixties such as *Ruth and Boaz* (1855), *The Rose Garden* (1860-61), *Love's Greeting* (c.1861), and, most notably, *The Wedding of Saint George and the Princess Sabra* (1857). To an extent the comic counterpart of *Chapel before the Lists* and the earthly equivalent of the final stanzas of "The Staff and Scrip," this last watercolour depicts the Saint after he has destroyed a manifestation of the forces of evil (the dragon) and thus earned the hand of the Princess. With his head surrounded by the nimbus of his sainthood, he embraces and kisses his bride, who has left her chair to kneel before him where he is seated in an ornately decorated throne and with a pair of scissors cuts the lock of her hair that she has affixed to his armour.[27] Above the embracing couple, at the top and centre of the picture space, hangs a golden crown, a traditional emblem of earthly power and heavenly reward whose position partly inside and partly outside the border of the painting makes it a gesture in both directions. Beyond an aperture in the background, two angels ring a chime of golden bells and behind them a nuptial bed is plainly visible.[28] The very presence in the painting of angels as well as various mundane objects (a broom, a comb, a hairbrush) further suggests the coming together of the heavenly and the earthly. Described by James Smetham as "a golden dim dream [of] [l]ove 'credulous all gold,' gold armour, [and] a sense of secret enclosure in 'palace chambers far apart'" (the allusions are to Milton's translation of "The Fifth Ode of Horace, Lib. 1" and to Tennyson's description of Sleeping Beauty in "The Daydream"),[29] *The Wedding of Saint George and the Princess Sabra* is a pictorial epithalamium in which the saintly and the sexual are fully reconciled and blessed, not in heaven, but on earth.

Something of the same sense of reconciliation, also with a suggestion of marriage, can be found in *The Tune of the Seven Towers*, which was painted in the same year and the same medium (watercolour) as *The Wedding of Saint George and the Princess Sabra*.[30] Taking its title from the enormous Byzantine fortress (Yedikule) in Constantinople/Istanbul that was held by crusaders until the fall of the Eastern Roman Empire in 1453, *The Tune of the Seven Towers* depicts a young woman in a red dress with a pilgrim's cockle shell at the neck, sitting in a large chair and plucking the strings of a musical instrument that rests on her lap. A coronet on her trailing armband suggests that she is either royal or aristocratic. Leaning on his sword beside her, a young man listens intently and sadly to her affective "tune." Behind her, a woman also listens, but with a distraught expression, her head resting against the back of the chair and her hands clutched together as if in anguish. Above, a bell hangs immobile in a belfry, its green pull untouched by the listening woman. At the top right, a bird appears to be flying up the well of a circular staircase, an image of ascent towards the divine that appears in a number of Rossetti's works, including "Pax Vobis" (1850) and *Fra Pace* (1856). At the top left, a figure leans in at an aperture to place an orange branch, a traditional emblem of marriage, on a recessed bed. In *Chapel before the Lists* and *The Wedding of Saint George and the Princess Sabra*, the swords of the knight and the Saint (and, in the latter, the design of the black and white crest on the Saint's shoulder) lend diagonal elements to the design that come quite literally to the foreground in *The Tune of the Seven Towers* in the form of the staff from which hangs a pendant depicting the seven towers of the painting's title. The pendant also carries astronomical and floral figures whose placement in relation to the title and easy legibility as emblems suggest that they may provide a gloss on the painting's enigmatic scenario. Above and below the fortress are a stylized sun and moon, figures traditionally (and by Rossetti) associated with Christ (the Son) and the Virgin Mary. Within its walls are a lily and a rose, flowers that come bearing not just sacred significance from their association with Christ's mother but also sexual and sacred significance from their appearance in the Song of Songs 2:1 "I am the rose of Sharon, and the lily of the valleys." If there is any biographical significance to the fact that the woman playing the instrument in *The Tune of the Seven Towers* was modelled by Elizabeth Siddal,[31] then its pensive, even melancholy, mood might suggest that, despite its gestures towards the marriage of the sacred and the sexual, it is a work made in less than happy contemplation of the wedding that eventually took place after much delay and soul-searching on Rossetti's part on 23 May 1860.

There may also be biographical significance to the fact that the final appearance of the emblematic cockle shell in Rossetti's work is in the compositional study for the *Dantis Amor* (1860) that he intended for a settle in William Morris's Red House. In the background of the design, the heavens are divided diagonally along an axis inscribed with the closing line of the *Paradiso* "L'AMOR CHE MUOVE IL SOL E L'ALTRE STELLE": "THE LOVE THAT MOVES THE SUN AND THE OTHER STARS." From a radiant sun in the top, left corner, a crowned and stern-face Christ looks down past words from the closing sentence of the *Vita Nuova*: "QUI EST PER OMNIA SAECULA BENEDICTUS." Opposite him, in the bottom, right corner, a pensive and curiously bland and grumpy Beatrice looks out from the inner curve of a crescent moon inscribed with another part of the closing sentence of the *Vita Nuova*: "QUELLA BEATA BEATRICE CHE MIRA CONTINUAMENTE NELLE FACCIA DI COLLUI."[32] At the centre of the design, with half his body in the upper realm and half his body in the lower, stands a winged and sadly pensive figure that represents Dante's conception of Love (Amor), holding in his left hand the bow and arrow of Cupid (desire) and in his right a sundial pointing to the date and time of Beatrice's death. In his hat is the pilgrim's cockle shell in visual allusion to the last poem in the *Vita Nuova*, where Dante tropes his new way of thinking and seeing after the death of Beatrice as "a *'Pilgrim Spirit' because it goes up spiritually...like a pilgrim who is out of his own country*" (*CPP* 291-92). When Rossetti came to work up the design for *Dantis Amor* into the panel for the settle in the Red House that he left unfinished in the summer of 1860, the face of Beatrice became that of Jane Morris, who would soon become, if she had not already, his lover, and the focus of another phase of his pictorial and literary meditations on the relationships between and among life, love, death, and the afterlife.

From at least the time of the early versions of "The Blessed Damozel" in the eighteen forties to the few years that elapsed between his massive paintings of the poem (1875-78, 1875-79) and his death in 1882, Rossetti was continually fascinated by the idea that a sanctified earthly love might achieve fulfilment beyond the grave. Such a possibility was held dear by many Victorians and remains so today to many people who cherish a belief in the persistence of individual identity after death. In Dante Gabriel Rossetti's case, hope for reunification with the beloved in an afterlife was nurtured and periodically renewed and sustained by his deep attachment to the work of Dante. Rarely is this preoccupation more evident than in his poems and paintings of the eighteen fifties, including the literary ballad of considerable complexity that Evelyn Waugh regarded as "a narrative poem of immense vigour" and "perhaps the most completely successful" of the long poems in *Poems* (1870) (157): "The Staff and Scrip."

UNIVERSITY OF WESTERN ONTARIO

NOTES

1 In *Works* (1911), William Michael Rossetti notes that the "actual composition [of the poem] came somewhat later" and suggests 1851-52 as the likely time (649, xxxiii); however, in the *Collected Works* of 1886 and the *Poems* of 1904 he assigns the poem's composition to 1853 (see *Collected Works* 2:516 and *Poems* 1:217). The Humanities Research Center at the University of Texas holds two manuscripts of the poem, both of which are available in Jerome McGann, "Dante Gabriel Rossetti: a Hypermedia Research Archive" (The Rossetti Archive; hereafter *RA*). Designated Texas A and Texas B by Robert N. Keane in the only extensive use of them to date (see his *Dante Gabriel Rossetti: The Poet as Craftsman* 55-63), the two manuscripts consist of (A) seven holograph pages with numerous additions and deletions; and (B) a partial fair copy comprising three pages containing further additions and deletions. Neither is dated but if, as seems to be the case, they reflect Rossetti's preparation of the poem for publication in the December 1856 number of the *Oxford and Cambridge Magazine* (hereafter *OCM*) then the changes

that they contain were probably made during the period immediately preceding that date. The poem was again revised for publication in *Poems* (1870) (the epigraph and one stanza were omitted, nine stanzas were substantially revised, and numerous minor changes were made), and it was further revised for inclusion in the 1881 edition of *Poems* (three stanzas were added and several minor changes made). In his discussion of these three stages of revision, Keane observes that the overall effect of the changes, especially those of 1856, was to "eliminate unnecessary detail" such as "extraneous pieties" in order to enhance what he sees as the poem's central theme of "love triumphing over war and death." Since the present essay is primarily concerned with Rossetti's work of the eighteen fifties, the principal text cited is that of 1856. For ease of reference, however, parallel citations are given to the 1881 text in Jerome McGann's edition of Rossetti's *Collected Poetry and Prose* (hereafter *CPP*) where, it needs to be noted, the poem's title is erroneously given as "The Staff and the Scrip."

2 Florence Saunders Boos comments that, if the poem was indeed written when William Michael Rossetti states, "it reveals Rossetti's handling of a chivalric theme ...before his encounter with Morris and contains themes and situations suggestive of Morris" (131). For the poem's Pre-Raphaelite pictorialism see the remarks of Oliver Elton later in this essay.

3 See also J.H. Heritage's edition of the *Gesta Romanorum*, where the same two tales in a Latin edition are credited with providing the "groundwork for Mr. D.G. Rossetti's poem 'The Scrip and the Staff' [sic]" (452n).

4 In the 1856 version of the poem, the Queen "would wake with a clear mind/That letters writ to calm/Her soul lay in the scrip; and find/Pink shells, a torpid balm,/And dust of palm" (775), but in *Poems* (1870 and 1881) she only "once woke with a clear mind/That letters writ to calm/Her soul lay in the scrip; to find/Only a torpid balm/And dust of palm" (55). The lines as first published were added when, as speculated in note 1, above, the poem was revised for publication in 1856.

5 See William Michael's Notes in *Works* 649-50 and James Stephens *et al* 1238-39. In *CPP*, McGann notes that "[t]he poem is based on one (and perhaps two) anecdotes from the *Gesta Romanorum*: no. 25 "Of Ingratitude" and no. 66 "Of Constancy," a point that he also makes in the section of "The Staff and Scrip" in *RA*. See also Keane 54-55 for a detailed discussion of Rossetti's amalgamation of materials from the two tales.

6 See "The Staff and Scrip" in Texas B (*RA* [page (7)].

7 See "St. Luke the Painter," the first sonnet in Rossetti's "Old and New Art" group of 1840-49 (*CPP* 160) and D.M.R. Bentley, "Rossetti's Pre-Raphaelite Manifesto."

8 In title, name, and attributes Queen Blanchelys recalls "White Queen Blanche, like a queen of lilies,/With a voice like any mermaiden" in François Villon's "A Ballad of Dead Ladies" (*CPP* 119), which, however, Rossetti did not translate until 1869. Lionel Stevenson observes that "Blanchelys...implies an Old French setting, but otherwise...the action [of 'The Staff and Scrip'] could take place anywhere in medieval Europe" (61). A reader familiar with Villon's original "Ballade des dames du temps jadis" would also recall that "La royne Blanche comme ung lys... chantoit a voix de sereine" (38)—"sings with the voice of a siren."

9 See also Rossetti's "The Sin of Detection" (1848), where the same combination is used to describe a scorned and shameful woman who is nevertheless treated with respect by the poem's speaker: "Both her white breasts heaved/Like heaving water with their weight of lace;/And her long tresses, full of musk and myrrh,/Were shaken from the braid her fingers weaved..." (*Works* 263).

10 In a stanza that was deleted prior to publication in 1856, the identity of the Pilgrim as a "Palmer" is reinforced by the statement that "No vassal sued [him] for slips of palm" (Texas A, *RA* page [1b]).

11   Although Rossetti's conception of Love as a pilgrim probably had its principal source in Dante (more of which later), it may also have roots in *Le Roman de la rose*, a few lines of which he translated in 1850 (see *Works* 537 and xxxv) and to which he returned for inspiration in the early 'sixties (see Surtees 126 [*Love's Greeting* (c.1861) and the 1864 replica entitled *Roman de la Rose*). It may also have been nourished by the Baron de la Motte Fouqué's *Minstrel Love* (trans. 1845), a favourite book of Morris and Burne-Jones at Oxford (see Burne-Jones 1:141), where several engravings by Edward Corbould depict the protagonist, a troubadour minstrel and lover, as a pilgrim complete with "cockle-hat," staff, and scrip.   There is no evidence that Rossetti knew *Minstrel Love*, but there can be little doubt that its story of two lovers who are likened to Christ and the Virgin and who are reunited in Heaven would have greatly appealed to him.

12   The "stalls" of this line, which becomes "But with imperishable peace" in subsequent versions (*CPP* 24), come with religious as well as chivalric associations in accordance with the *OED* definition of a stall as "[a] fixed seat enclosed either wholly or partially, at the back and sides, esp[ecially] each of a row of seats in the choir of a church for the use of the clergy or [the] religious...; also, each of the seats appropriated to knights of the higher orders of chivalry (e.g. the Knights of the Garter in St. George's Chapel, Windsor...)" In her description of the heavenly city in Henry Francis Cary's translation of *Paradiso*, 30, Beatrice explains to Dante that the "proud stall" over which a crown is "Suspended" is awaiting the arrival of Emperor Henry VII (131-37). Keane suggests that "[p]erhaps choir 'stalls' seemed too close to stable stalls, and stalls, even when contiguous, serve to separate the heavenly lovers" (60-61).

13   The presentation of the exchanges between the Pilgrim and the Queen may reflect Rossetti's reading of the *The Thornton Romances* (1844), a copy of which was in his library circa 1866 (see William Michael Rossetti, "Books"). Indeed, echoes of content as well as form are raised in "The Staff and Scrip" by such stanzas as the following (numbers 49 and 63) in "The Romance of Sir Isumbras," a favourite of the second generation of Pre-Raphaelites:

> The riche qwene in haulle was sett,
> Knyghttes hir serves to handes fete,
>   Were clede in robis of palle;
> In the floure a clothe was layde,
> "This povre palmere," the stewarde sayde,
>   "Salle sytt abowene zow alle."
> Mete and drynke was forthe broghte,
> Sir Ysambrace sett and ete noghte,
>   But luked abowte in the haulle.
> So mekille he sawe of gamene and glee,
> And thoughte what he was sonnt to be,
>   And terys lete he falle.
>   . . .
> Sir Ysambrace was thane fulle was,
> He kyssede his lady and wolde furthe gaa
>   With sorow and hert fulle sare;
> A dolefulle worde thane gunne he saye,
> "Nowe, certis, lady, hafe now gud daye,
>   For nowe and evermare!"
> "A! lorde," scho sayd, "helpe that I were dyghte
> In armours, als I were a knyghte,
>   And with the wille I fare;

And God that made bothe see and lande,
My saule I wyte into thy hande,
    For I kepe to lyffe no more!" (111, 118).

14 In a deleted portion of the poem in Texas A, the Pilgrim-knight's vow is given as "to shield/Even with his life the truth," and the purpose of his pilgrimage is also stated: "he sought/To win for the dear soul [of his dead brother]/Its aureole" (*RA* pages 3 and 3a). J.C. Earle suggests that his vow was "to defend wronged innocence" (270), but there is no evidence for this either in the manuscript or in the published versions of the poem.

15 According to Texas A, after learning of the plight of Queen Blanchelys, the Pilgrim "stood and prayed within himself," and in subsequent stanzas more detailed evidence of his piety is provided than in the published versions: on arriving in the city where the Queen's "court" is located, he "kneel[s] in prayer" in an "empty" church, asks a priest to "take...[his] shrift" (hear his confession), and receives "benison" (blessing) from an "aged priest" (*RA* pages 1,[1a], [1b]). In Texas B, the stanzas in which the "aged priest" offers "benison" and the Pilgrim requests "shrift" are brought together so that there is only one priest [page (3)].) When the Queen asks him who will praise him if he is killed, he answers "'Christ'" and, later, she describes his soul as "assoilzied"—that is, absolved from sin (*RA* pages 2 and 6). Although the *Oxford and Cambridge Magazine* and *Poems* (1870) versions of the poem contain several historically appropriate references to Catholic practices and forms of worship (for example, while the Queen and her ladies await the return of the knight, "anthem[s]" and "chaunts" are sung [*OCM* 773-74, 52-53]), the poem's Catholic context is more pronounced in both the manuscript and in the *Poems* (1881) versions: in the former, the first priest gives the Pilgrim absolution in Latin ("'Son, *in hoc nomine*/*Asolvo te*—'") and the "watchers" awaiting his return are so "Dizzy with fast" that the "oriel-panes" and "gilded seraphim" in the chapel "shift and swim in their eyes" (*RA* pages [1b] and 4); and in the latter the stanza containing the reference to fasting is reintroduced, as is another stanza that appears in the manuscript, but not in the *OCM* or *Poems* (1870) versions:

    The Queen is pale, her maidens ail;
       And to the organ-tones
    They sing but faintly, who sang well
       The matin-orisons,
         The lauds and nones (*CPP* 21).

The removal and restoration of religious materials is consistent with the overall pattern placed on view in Bentley, "From Allegory to Indeterminacy."

16 In Texas A, it is the Pilgrim's dead brother's "face" that "he saw weep/Each night throughout his dream/...confused in sleep/With visages supreme/Not known to him" (*RA*, page 3a) and in *Poems* (1870 and 1881) he sees the "Queen's...face" "Each night through every dream" (*CPP* 20), an intensification of concentration on the female face that is also reflected in Rossetti's paintings from the late 'fifties onwards.

17 In *Poems* (1870 and 1881) "she would wake" becomes "once she woke" and what she finds is "Only a torpid balm/And dust of palm" (*CPP* 23). In a letter to William Michael of 26 August 1869, Rossetti recalls that he "had made additions (now lost) at points which...[he] thought abrupt in...*Staff & Scrip*...something...where the damsel gives her the relics to develop this incident & help the transition" (4:248).

18 When viewed from the psychoanalytical perspective of Sigmund Freud's distinction between "mourning" and "melancholia" and the literature on "introjection" and "incorporation" to which it has given rise, the process of mourning enables Queen Blanchelys to accept (introject) the loved object and thus to lead a happy life. A failure to mourn fully would have resulted in the internalization of the loved object as an

idealized spectre in the ego (incorporation) and thus in melancholia or depression. See Freud, Eugenio Donato 202-07, and Nicolas Abraham and Maria Torok.

19 It is almost unnecessary to point out that the reunion of Queen Blanchelys with the Pilgrim-knight in Heaven recalls the Assumption of the Virgin Mary, which, as Anna Jameson observes in *Legends of the Madonna*, "traditionally takes place in the court of heaven [with] its argent fields" (24).

20 In *Typology of Scripture* (1845-47), a book that Rossetti may have consulted in conceiving his avowedly typological *The Passover of the Holy Family* (1855-56), Patrick Fairbairn justifies the conception of "God as a *jealous* being" in the second Commandment against the "railing accusations" of "avowed infidels and rationalistic divines" that it is "peculiarly Jewish" and "flagrantly obnoxious to right principle" by observing that "every scholar knows that the word in the original is by no means restricted to what is distinctively meant by jealousy, and that the radical and proper idea ... has respect merely to the zeal or ardor with which any one is disposed to vindicate his own rights. Applied to God, it simply presents him to our view as the one Supreme Jehovah, who as such claims—can not indeed but claim—... the undivided love and homage of His creatures, and who, consequently, must resist with holy zeal and indignation every attempt to deprive Him of what is so peculiarly His own. It is only to give vividness to this idea, by investing it with the properties of an earthly relation, that the divine affection is so often presented under the special form of jealousy" (2:102).

21 Boos comments that "[t]he close identification of the agent of violence with passion" in the Pilgrim-knight "suggest[s] Morris" (131); and see Bentley, "William Morris' 'The Wind'" for a discussion of sexual frustration as an apparent cause of self-destruction, a pattern found elsewhere in *The Defence of Guenevere, and Other Poems*, for instance in "Golden Wings."

22 A fifth panel would be the reunion of the Queen and Pilgrim-knight in Heaven.

23 *Before the Battle* (1857-58), which depicts a lady attaching a pennant to a knight's halberd against a background of warriors in armour and women working at looms, belongs to the same thematic cluster as *Chapel before the Lists,* as does Burne-Jones' *The Knight's Farewell* (1858). See Surtees 99 and 106 and Martin Harrison and Bill Walters 30.

24 See Bentley, "Seroux D'Agincourt's *Histoire*" for a discussion of *Fra Pace* in relation to its context and possible sources.   25 It is quite possible that when he was painting *Chapel before the Lists* Rossetti had in mind Ruskin's lengthy discussion and illustration of the differences between a "true" ("Lombard-Gothic") and "false" ("classic [Roman]") gryphon in his chapter on the grotesque in *Modern Painters* 3, for in 1855 he made water colours of subjects from Dante that were chosen by Ruskin and are discussed in the volume (see my "D.G. Rossetti's Ruskinian Watercolours"). An "honest imagination" will create a "true" gryphon, asserts Ruskin, because it "has its griffinism, and grace, and usefulness...but the false composer, caring for nothing but himself and his rules, loses everything,—the griffinism, grace, and all" (3:111; and see 3:106-12 and 4:230 and 254). If not deliberately then coincidentally, the gryphon in *Chapel before the Lists* bears a closer resemblance to Ruskin's "Lombard-Gothic" gryphon than to his "classical (Roman)" one.

26 A helmet surmounted by a gryphon's head also appears in the later *Saint George and the Princess Sabra* (1861-62), where it is somewhat improbably used as the container for the water in which the saint is washing his hands after slaying the dragon.

27 Taken together, the golden armour of St George and the grotesque head of the dragon that he has slain recall Ingres' *Ruggiero and Angelica* (or *Roger Freeing Angelica*), the highly theatrical illustration of Ariosto's *Orlando Furioso* to which Rossetti responded

with two sonnets when he and William Holman Hunt saw it in the Louvre in the autumn of 1849. The diagonal axis provided by Ruggiero's lance in Ingres' painting may have influenced the design of *The Tune of the Seven Towers*, which is shortly to be discussed above. It was not until January 1865 that Rossetti recorded his admiration for Carpaccio's St George series in the Scuola di San Giorgio degli Schiavoni in Venice (see *Correspondence* 3:237), but if this began before 1857 the depiction of the Saint's armour and the dragon's head in *The Wedding of Saint George and the Princess Sabra* may be indebted to Carpaccio. Certainly, a clawed snout is a feature shared by the dragons of both artists. Rossetti's decision to depict only the dragon's head may reflect Ruskin's commentary on the merits of representing only a part rather than the whole of a dragon's body in *Modern Painters* 2:165-66.

28 The bed bears a remote resemblance to the one in Jan Van Eyck's *The Arnolfini Marriage* (or, as it is now known, *The Portrait of Giovanni(?) Arnolfini and His Wife Giovanna Cenani*), which Rossetti had seen and admired in the National Gallery by October 1849 (see *Correspondence* 1:128).

29 "[B]ut quaint chambers in quaint palaces," continues Smetham, "where angels creep in through sliding panel doors, and stand behind rows of flowers, drumming on golden bells, with wings crimson and green. There...[is] also a queer remnant of a dragon's head...the glazed eye [of] which somehow seem[s] to wink at the spectator, as much as to say, 'Do you believe in St. George and the Dragon? If you do, I don't. But do you think we mean *nothing,* the man in gold and I? Either way I pity you, my friend'" (qtd. in Surtees 97).

30 In March 1864, after he had arranged for the sale of eight of his water-colours to George Rae, Rossetti sent him a plan for hanging them to their "greatest effect" that places *The Tune of the Seven Towers* (left), *Chapel before the Lists* (centre), and *The Wedding of Saint George and the Princess Sabra* (right) on one tier and thus links them by spatial as well as thematic association (*Correspondence* 3:128-29, and see 3:116-17). Most of the paintings had originally belonged to Morris, who, of course, wrote poems inspired by *The Tune of the Seven Towers* and *The Blue Closet*. "[T]he poems were the result of the pictures," Rossetti would explain in December 1872, "but they don't at all tally to my purpose with them, though beautiful in themselves" (5:364).

31 Alastair Grieve suggests that "the subject [of *The Tune of the Seven Towers*] is partly autobiographical," adding that "[d]uring this period Rossetti considered marrying Elizabeth Siddal but was depressed by her illness which was thought to be fatal. She posed for the woman dressed in red...and she wears a scallop shell at her neck—a symbol of pilgrimage and a possible reference to her travels in search of health."

32 In Rossetti's translation, the closing sentence of the *Vita Nuova* reads: "After the which, may it seem good unto Him who is the Master of Grace, that my spirit should go hence to behold the glory of his lady: to wit, of that blessed Beatrice who now gazeth continually on His countenance *qui est per omnia saecula benedictus* [who is blessed throughout all ages]" (*CPP* 292).

WORKS CITED

Abraham, Nicolas, and Maria Torok. *The Wolf Man's Magic Word: A Cryptonomy.* Trans. Nicholas Rand. Theory and History of Literature 37. Minneapolis: University of Minnesota Press, 1986.

Alighieri, Dante. *The Vision; or, Hell, Purgatory, and Paradise.* Trans. Henry Francis Cary. 1814. 3rd ed. 1844 London: Frederick Warne, n.d.

Bentley, D.M.R. "D.G. Rossetti's Ruskinian Watercolours of 1855." *Journal of Pre-Raphaelite Studies* n.s. 14 (Fall 2005): 17-29.

_____. "From Allegory to Indeterminacy: Dante Gabriel Rossetti's Positive Agnosticism." *Dalhousie Review* 70 (Spring 1990): 70-106 and 70 (Summer 1990): 146-68.

_____. "Rossetti's Pre-Raphaelite Manifesto: The 'Old and New Art' Sonnets." *English Language Notes* 15.3 (Mar 1978): 197-203.

_____. "Seroux D'Agincourt's *Histoire* as a Possible Point of Departure for Two Pictures by Dante Gabriel Rossetti and Some Contingent Observations." *Journal of Pre-Raphaelite Studies*, ns 11 (Fall 2002): 33-42.

_____. "William Morris' 'The Wind.'" *Trivium* 13 (Summer 1978): 31-37.

Boos, Florence Saunders. *The Poetry* of Dante G. Rossetti: *A Critical Reading and Source Study.* The Hague and Paris: Mouton, 1976.

Brown, Ford Madox. *Diary.* Ed. Virginia Surtees. New Haven: Yale UP, 1981.

B[urne]-J[ones], G[eorgiana]. *Memorials of Edward Burne-Jones.* 2 vols. London: Macmillan, 1904.

Donato, Eugenio. *The Script of Decadence: Essays on the Fictions of Flaubert and the Poetics of Romanticism.* New York and Oxford: Oxford UP, 1993.

[Earle, J.C.]. "Rossetti's Poems." *Catholic World* 19 (May 1874): 263-72.

Fairbairn, Patrick. *Typology of Scripture.* 1900. Grand Rapids, Michigan: Kregel Publications, 1989.

Freud, Sigmund. "Mourning and Melancholia." In *Complete Psychoanalytical Works.* By Sigmund Freud. ed. James Strachey. 24 vols. London: Hogarth Press and Institute of Psycho-Analysis, 1955. 14A: 237-58.

Gesta Romanorum; or, Entertaining Moral Stories. Trans. Charles Swan. 2 vols. London: C. and J. Rivington. 1824.

Gesta Romanorum; or, Entertaining Moral Stories. Trans. Charles Swan. Ed. J.H. Heritage. London: G. Bell and Son, 1877.

Grieve, Alastair. "The Tune of the Seven Towers." *The Pre-Raphaelites.* Catalogue for the Exhibition at the Tate Gallery, 7 March - 28 May, 1984. London: Tate Gallery: Penguin Books, 1984. 281.

Halliwell, James Orchard. *The Thornton Romances. The Early English Metrical Romances of Perceval, Isumbras, Eglamour, and Degrevant.* London: Camden Society, 1844.

Harrison, Martin, and Bill Watters. *Burne-Jones.* London: Barrie and Jenkins, 1973.

Hough, Graham. *The Last Romantics.* London: Duckworth, 1949.

Howard, Ronnalie Roper. *The Dark Glass: Vision and Technique in the Poetry of Dante Gabriel Rossetti.* [Athens]: Ohio UP, 1972.

Jameson, A[nna] B[rownell]. *Legends of the Madonna.* 1852. 3rd ed. London: Longman, Green, Longman, Roberts, and Green, 1864.

Keane, Robert N. *Dante Gabriel Rossetti: The Poet as Craftsman.* Studies in Nineteenth-Century British Literature 17. New York: Peter Lang, 2002.

Knight, Joseph. *Life of Dante Gabriel Rossetti.* London: Scott, 1887.

Masefield, John. *Thanks before Going: Notes on Some of the Original Poems of Dante Gabriel Rossetti.* London: William Heinemann, 1946.

McGann, Jerome, ed. "Dante Gabriel Rossetti: A Hypermedia Research Archive." http://www.rossettiarchive.org

Mégroz, R.L. *Dante Gabriel Rossetti, Painter Poet of Heaven in Earth.* London: Faber, 1928.

The Old English Versions of the Gesta Romanorum. Ed. Sir Frederic Madden. Roxburgh Club. London: W. Nicol, Shakespeare Press, 1838.

Pater, Walter. *Appreciations, with an Essay on Style*. 1889. London: Macmillan, 1924.

Rossetti, Dante Gabriel. *Collected Poetry and Prose*. Ed. Jerome McGann. New Haven and London: Yale UP, 2003.

_____. *Correspondence of Dante Gabriel Rossetti*. Ed. William E. Fredeman. 7 vols (to date). Cambridge: D.S. Brewer, 2002-05.

_____. *Poems*. London: F.S. Ellis, 1870.

_____. "The Staff and Scrip." *Oxford and Cambridge Magazine* 12 (Dec. 1856): 771-75.

_____. *Works*. Ed. William M. Rossetti. London: Ellis, 1911.

Ruskin, John. *Modern Painters*. 1843-60. 6 vols. Orpington: George Allen, 1888.

Sarrazin, Gabriel. *Poètes modernes de l'Angleterre*. Paris: Ollendorff, 1885.

Stephens, James, Edwin L. Beck and Royall H. Snow, eds. *Victorian and Later English Poets*. 1934. New York: American Book Company, 1949.

Stevenson, Lionel. *The Pre-Raphaelite Poets*. Chapel Hill: U of North Carolina P, 1972.

Surtees, Virginia. *The Paintings and Drawings of Dante Gabriel Rossetti (1828-1882): A Catalogue Raisonné*. Oxford: Clarendon Press, 1971.

Villon, François. *Oeuvres complètes*. Ed. Louis Moland. Paris: Librairie Garnier Frèves, n.d.

Waugh, Evelyn. *Rossetti: His Life and Works*. London: Duckworth, 1928.

www.ingramcontent.com/pod-product-compliance
Lightning Source LLC
Chambersburg PA
CBHW051840020726
47502CB00005B/1873